Parenting in Planned Lesbian Families

Omslagontwerp: René Staelenberg, Amsterdam
Vormgeving: Klaas Hulshof, Maarssen

ISBN 90 5629 367 2
NUR 847

© Vossiuspers UvA, Amsterdam 2004

# Parenting in Planned Lesbian Families

ACADEMISCH PROEFSCHRIFT

ter verkrijging van de graad van doctor
aan de Universiteit van Amsterdam
op gezag van Rector Magnificus
prof. mr. P. F. van der Heijden
ten overstaan van een door het college van promoties ingestelde
commissie, in het openbaar te verdedigen in de Aula der Universiteit
op woensdag 8 december 2004, te 10:00

door

## Henrica Maria Wilhelmina Bos

geboren te Valkenswaard

Vossiuspers UvA

**Promotiecommissie:**

| | |
|---|---|
| Promotor: | prof. dr. D.C. van den Boom |
| Copromotor: | dr. F. van Balen |

| | |
|---|---|
| Overige leden: | prof. dr. D.D.M. Braat |
| | prof. dr. W. Everaerd |
| | prof. dr. J. Hermanns |
| | dr. Th.G.M. Sandfort |
| | prof. dr. L.W.C. Tavecchio |

| | |
|---|---|
| Faculteit: | Faculteit der Maatschappij- en Gedragswetenschappen |

# Contents

# I

# Parenting in Planned Lesbian Families

For decades, theory and research on family functioning focused on two-parent families consisting of a father and a mother. Over the past 30 years, however, the concept of what makes a "family" has changed dramatically. Some children now grow up in a "patchwork" or "blended" family, that is, a family comprising two parents, one of whom has a new partner who has a child or children from a previous relationship. Other children grow up in a "planned lesbian family," that is, a family headed by two lesbian mothers who decided to have children together. These later families are a recent phenomenon, and they differ from lesbian families whose children were born into a previous, heterosexual relationship. Investigating planned lesbian families is a new area of research on family functioning (Parke, 2004).

The right and fitness of lesbians to parent is widely disputed in the media, the legal and policy arena, and in the social sciences. Opponents of lesbian parenting claim that the children of lesbian parents run the risk of developing a variety of behavior problems, because they are raised fatherless and/or because they lack a biological tie with one of the mothers (Blankenhorn, 1995; Cameron & Cameron, 1996; Cameron, Cameron, & Landess, 1996; Wardle, 1997). Advocates of same-sex marriages and lesbian parenthood rely on the few studies that have been conducted with planned lesbian families. Based on these studies, they argue that there is no evidence to support the proposition that only the traditional, nuclear mother-father family is the ideal environment in which to raise children.

However, several scholars have pointed out the scientific limitations of the social science literature on planned lesbian parenting (Stacey & Biblarz, 2001). For example, most findings are based on relatively small samples, most of which were recruited either from hospital fertility departments or from friendship networks. Another methodological critique is that most studies compare families headed by a single lesbian to families headed by a single heterosexual. Finally, many studies rely on maternal self-reports of their parenting skills and abilities, rather than on observations of the parent-child relationship. In the investigations reported in this thesis, these methodological shortcomings were addressed by examining a large sample of planned lesbian families, which had been recruited in several ways, and by comparing them with two-parent heterosexual families.

Research on lesbian/planned lesbian families proceeds from two scientific perspectives, *viz.* family research, and lesbian and gay studies. In both perspectives, lesbian families are a relatively new phenomenon.

*Family research.* For decades, most researchers and theorists in the field of family research have concentrated on investigating parental influences on the development of children. Also, the focus is mainly on traditional families, *viz.* two-parent families in which the mother is a full-time homemaker and care provider, and the father is primarily the breadwinner. Recently, however, a few studies have paid attention to planned lesbian families. In general, no differences have been observed in child rearing or child development between lesbian families and heterosexual families. It has been established, however, that lesbian social mothers score significantly higher on the quality of parenting awareness skills (Flaks, Ficher, Masterpasqua, & Joseph, 1995) and on parent child interaction (Brewaeys, Ponjaert, van Hall, & Golombok, 1997; Golombok, Tasker, & Murray, 1997) than heterosexual fathers do. Critics state that the majority of these studies are based on the no-difference hypothesis (Clarke, 2002; Stacey & Biblarz, 2001), and thus emphasize similarities in parenting between lesbian and heterosexual families. Studies have failed to unravel the family processes in which lesbian and heterosexual families differ. Lesbian and heterosexual families possibly differ in several respects, as a result of special circumstances. For lesbian women, for example, getting pregnant is more complex than it is for fertile heterosexual couples. Furthermore, lesbian parents have to cope with less favorable attitudes toward lesbian parenting. There are also indications that the division of professional employment, practical activities, and household activities between parents in lesbian families is more equal than it is in heterosexual families (Brewaeys, Ponjaert, van Hall, & Golombok, 1997). Research on lesbian parents needs to pay more attention to these differences, and to the consequences they may have for the parent-child relationship. Are potential differences related to the division of parenting and occupational tasks, the unique circumstances of getting pregnant through reproductive help, and/or to being a lesbian mother in a society less favorable toward lesbian motherhood? In the investigations reported here, it was examined whether lesbian and heterosexual families differ in these respects, and if so, what the consequences of these differences are for child rearing.

*Lesbian and gay studies.* The perspectives on homosexuality in the social sciences can be divided into several categories (Sandfort, 2000). The first perspective was pathological, while the second stressed the normality of homosexuality. Later, gay and lesbian affirmative psychology arose as an alternative to these traditional approaches. In this view, the focus is on a range of aspects of gay and lesbian lives. Psychological research into homosexuality has paid attention to such topics as the psychological functioning of gay men and lesbian women, becoming and being gay/lesbian, intimate relationships, and lesbian families. Most studies on lesbian women and their children have focused on whether lesbians can be good parents and whether they should be granted legal parenthood (Sandfort, 2000).

A variety of research designs are used in research on homosexuality (Sandfort, 2000). Several studies use a comparative design, and compare homosexual and heterosexual samples. In other inquiries, the focus is on issues specific to gays or to lesbians. Data are collected from gay and lesbian persons only, with the aim of assessing the role played by variables related to homosexuality (e.g., negative treatment because of the person's sexual orientation) in such issues as psychological well being and quality of life. Negative treatment resulting from being a homosexual can be considered to be a stressor. Several authors label such experiences of homosexual men and lesbian women as 'minority stress' (Brooks, 1981; DiPlacido, 1998; Meyer, 1995, 2003a, 2003b). The influence of minority stress on lesbian women and gay men has been examined in various studies (Sandfort, Bos, & Vet, in press; Sandfort & Bos, 2000; Waldo, 1999). However, planned lesbian families have not previously been examined from the perspective of minority stress.

This thesis is unique because a combination of issues important in family studies and gay and lesbian studies are investigated, *viz.* (1) potential differences between lesbian families and heterosexual families, and its consequences on parenting and child development, and (2) minority stress and its consequences on child development and experiences of parenthood.
The following four issues are central to this thesis:
- Parenthood motivation and the desire to have children
- The experience of parenthood, couple relationship, social support, and child rearing goals
- Parental behavior and child development
- Minority stress and its relation to experiences of parenthood and child adjustment

*Parenthood motivation and the desire to have children.* During their transition to parenthood, lesbian women may be confronted with questions posed by their family, friends, and other persons in their environment (e.g., colleagues). In addition, lesbian women must deal with complex circumstances if they wish to become pregnant: they are in need of reproductive help. These circumstances force lesbian women to reflect carefully on their desire to have children. Because the desire and motivation to have children are assumed to affect parenting and the parent-child relationship (Colpin, 1994; Colpin, De Munter, & Vandemeulebroecke, 1998; Golombok, 1992; Van Balen & Trimbos-Kemper, 1995), it was examined whether, and if so how, the desire to have children and the reasons for having children differ from those of heterosexual parents.

*Experience of parenthood, couple relationship, social support, and child rearing goals.* Although the number of planned lesbian families has increased in recent years, these families are still social pioneers since lesbian mothers have to cope with less favorable attitudes toward lesbian motherhood. In this respect, lesbian families differ from heterosexual families, and this may affect the lives of lesbian mothers. We examined whether, and if so how, lesbian parents experience their parenthood, relationship, social support, and child rearing goals and how these differ from the way heterosexual parents experience such matters.

*Parental behavior and child development.* Several authors assume that lesbian families create new kinds of family characteristics, and that these have fascinating consequences for the parent-child relationship and child development (Dunne, 2000; Patterson, 1995a; Stacey & Biblarz, 2001). Previous research revealed some differences in child rearing between lesbian and heterosexual parents, however, without examining possible mediating variables, such as the division of family tasks, the desire to have children, and other aspects that are assumed to influence the parent-child relationship (i.e., the experience of parenthood and child rearing goals).

*Minority stress and its relation to experiences of parenthood and child adjustment.* Compared to other countries, the Netherlands provides a relatively positive climate for lesbian women (and gay men) (Inglehart, 1990; Sociaal Cultureel Planbureau, 2000; Sandfort, 1998; Waaldijk, 1993; Widmer, Treas, & Newcomb, 1998). Nevertheless, less favorable attitudes toward lesbians, gay men, and lesbian/gay families can also be observed (De Graaf & Sandfort, 2001). Such experiences of lesbian women (and gay men) have been defined as minority stress (Brooks, 1981; DiPlacido, 1998; Meyer, 1995, 2003a, 2003b). It is assumed that lesbian mothers who suffer more from minority stress experience parenthood as more stressful and feel a stronger need to justify the quality of their parenthood. Furthermore, it assumed that the children of a lesbian mother who experiences minority stress are less well adjusted.

As noted, this thesis combines two scientific perspectives of family research, and lesbian and gay studies. Methodological aspects that make our study exceptional is the use of multiple sources of data collection (standardized questionnaires, observations, diary methods), and planned lesbian families were recruited in several ways. Our sample comprised 100 planned lesbian families and 100 heterosexual families, making it the largest study on planned lesbian families ever performed.

## Organization of the thesis

Chapter II provides a review of research on lesbian families. Chapter III presents the findings of a study on lesbian and heterosexual parenthood motives and the desire to have children. Chapter IV compares mothers in planned lesbian families with fathers and mothers in heterosexual families on variables, such as experiences of parenthood, child rearing goals, and couple relationship. Chapter V reports on an investigation into differences in aspects of the parent-child relationship and child adjustment between lesbian families and heterosexual families. When differences between lesbian families and heterosexual families were found, it was also examined which variables accounted for these differences. Chapter VI focuses on lesbian families and their experiences with negative attitudes toward their non-traditional family situation, their own attitude toward being a lesbian, and its relation with experiences of parenthood and child adjustment. Chapter VII summarizes and discusses the most important findings.

# II

# Lesbian families and family functioning:
# An overview*

*In a literature search 44 published articles were identified reporting results in the field of lesbian parenthood, such as children's sexual identity, emotional/ behavioral development, social relationships and cognitive functioning, and maternal psychological health and parenting skills. This paper presents and discusses major findings on two family types: (1) lesbian families whose children were born in a previous heterosexual relationship, and (2) lesbian families whose children were born in the same-sex couple (planned lesbian families).*

## 2.1 Introduction

Lesbian families are a relatively new phenomenon in our society. In recent years, the concept of what makes a family has changed and in many of today's Western societies there are a variety of family types. Nowadays, some children are growing up in a one-parent rather than in a traditional mother-and-father family. Other children are growing up in a 'patchwork' or 'blended' family, because after divorce one of the parents found a new partner who had children out of a former relationship and together they have created a new family. In addition, more and more parents are choosing for co-parenting after a separation. Another type of non-traditional family is the two-mother lesbian family. The aim of this article is to provide an overview of existing studies on lesbian parenthood.

In the past, most women who were attracted to other women faced enormous societal pressure to marry a man and have children, and they had to repress their sexual feelings for women or to express them in a highly secretive way (Slater, 1999; Golombok, 2000). As a result of the gay liberation movement of the 1970s, increasing numbers of lesbians have abandoned secrecy. Lesbian women who were a parent in a heterosexual relationship came out of the closet and openly identified themselves as lesbians (Blumenfeld & Raymond, 1988). In the 1970s, these lesbian women began to fight for the custody of their children after divorce.

As a result of the increasing tolerance of homosexuality, an increasing number of women become after coming out as a lesbian. Some of these are single mothers, while others are couples who planned their family together and share the parenting role (Golombok, 2000). In the literature these families are characterized as

---

* This paper was presented at the national meeting of school counselors of the NVIH/COC, November, 1th, 2003, Utrecht, the Netherlands and is based on: Bos, H.M.W., Van Balen, F. & Van Den Boom, D.C. (in press). Patient, Eductaion and Counseling.

'planned lesbian families' (Golombok, 2000). This is in contrast to lesbian families whose children had been born to the mother in a previous heterosexual relationship before coming came out of the closet. It is difficult to say how many planned lesbian families there are; however, several social scientists made estimates (Patterson & Friel, 2000). In the US, for example, the number of lesbians who became a mother, after coming out as a lesbian, was in 1990 estimated as 5,000-10,000 (Patterson & Friel, 2000). In the Netherlands, it is estimated that there are 21,000 cohabiting lesbian couples, and that almost 15% of these couples have children (Steenhof & Harmsen, 2002, 2003). In autumn 2001, a Kaiser Family Foundation survey of 405 randomly selected, self-identified lesbians, gays and bisexuals in the US indicated that 8% of the respondents was a parent or legal guardian of a child under 18 who lived in their home (Kaiser Family Foundation, 2001). Among those lesbians, gays and bisexuals who were not parents at the time of the survey, almost half (49%) indicated that they would like to have children of their own some time. Regardless of the estimates, it is evident that a large number of children are growing up in lesbian families (Parke, 2004), and several authors have characterized this increase in children in planned lesbian families as a baby boom among lesbians (Patterson, 1995b; Morningstar, 1999).

As a result of the introduction of same-sex marriage and the legal recognition of lesbian parenthood (the non-biological mother can legally adopt the children born in the lesbian relationship), the Netherlands has become one of the most liberal countries in this respect (Maxwell, 2001; Van De Meerendonk & Scheepers, in press). However, public opinion in the Netherlands still holds that a traditional rather than a lesbian or gay family is the ideal environment in which to raise children (Van Der Avort, Cuypers, & De Hoog, 1996), and dominant public opinion is not in favor of equal rights for lesbians when it comes to adoption (Van De Meerendonk & Scheepers in press). In other countries, there are less favorable attitudes towards lesbian motherhood (King & Black 1999).

During the last 30 years, lesbian families have been of special interest in a number of contexts, such as the legal and policy arena, in the media and in empirical research (Clarke, 2002). Arguments against lesbian parenting have focused on the absence of a father, the homosexual orientation of the mother, and their negative consequences on the development of the children (Blankenhorn, 1995; Cameron & Cameron, 1996; Cameron, Cameron, & Landess, 1996; Wardle, 1997). Research on parenting and child rearing has repeatedly compared lesbian and heterosexual families, and in the last 30 years a growing body of studies on lesbian parents and the development of their children has been published. The purpose of this review is to describe the focus and context of the existing literature on lesbian parenthood, and to provide an overview of the results and research methods in this literature. A further objective is to outline challenges for future research on lesbian families.

## 2.2   Methods

Four computerized databases were identified studies for inclusion in this review of research on lesbian families, namely PschInfo, Educational Resources Information Centre (ERIC), Medline, and the Social Sciences Citation Index. Keywords were used in various combinations, namely lesbian women, lesbian mothers, lesbian families, children, child development, child outcomes, parenting, parental behavioral, child rearing, and parent-child relationship. Also the references of the collected articles were examined.

This systematic search yielded 44 studies on (1) lesbian families whose children had been born to the mother in a previous heterosexual relationship, and (2) lesbian families whose children had been born in the same-couple relationships (planned lesbian families). The studies selected in these two categories were assessed and categorized according to topic, sample and design, measures and main results (see Table 2.1 and 2.2). Unpublished studies were not included.

## 2.3   Results

### Focus and context of the studies

Concerns raised in custody disputes in which lesbian women fought for the custody of their children born in a heterosexual relationship were an important impetus for research on lesbian families. When custody or visitation rights were denied or curtailed, courts based their judgments on a lack of a male role model in lesbian families and on the inevitability of children being subject to bullying and social stigmatization (Patterson, 2002; Thompson, 2002). Judges assumed that the absence of a father combined with the presence of a lesbian mother would lead to atypical gender development in children. Boys were assumed to be less masculine in their identity and behavior and would grow up to be homosexual. Girls were supposed to be less feminine and would grow up to be lesbian. Judgments also included outcomes of reports that showed detrimental effects of the absence of a father on children's cognitive development. Another argument to deny custody was based on the idea that children having a lesbian mother would be teased, mobbed and/or ostracized by other children. As a consequence they would develop more psychological problems. Another argument to deny custody consisted of concern about the lesbian mothers, especially their child rearing behavior, the state of their mental health, and overall adjustment.

There was, however, a lack of empirical knowledge to base these judgments on. This lack of evidence prompted the first systematic studies on lesbian families. Initial research focused on the concerns raised in custody disputes, such as the development of children–especially their gender development and psychological adjustment–and the psychological health and well being of lesbian mothers (Patterson, 2002; Thompson, 2002). Research also focused on these issues in later studies of lesbian families whose children had been born to the lesbian couple (Sandfort & Bos 1998; Sandfort, 2000).

According to several authors (Sandfort, 2000; Stacey & Biblarz 2001), the implicit aim of these studies was to demonstrate that lesbian parents and their children are not different from heterosexual parents and their children, and that lesbian parents are no less successful or less worthy than heterosexual parents are. Against this background the studies on lesbian parenting were undertaken.

**Lesbian families with children born in a previous heterosexual relationship**
Twenty-three of the articles describe the results of studies of lesbian families whose children were born in a previous heterosexual relationship (see Table 2.1). In some studies, the sample consisted of either single – or two-mother lesbian families, while other studies focused on a combination of the two types of families. In most studies, families were compared with families consisting of single heterosexual mothers. However, a few studies reported different comparisons. One study compared divorced lesbian mothers with divorced gay fathers (Harris & Turner 1985), while another compared lesbian couples who had children with those who did not (Koepke, Hare, & Moran, 1992). In most studies, the data were collected using more or less structured interviews and self-administered questionnaires. Some studies exposed children to standardized material other than questionnaires in order to obtain their responses. In none of the studies were observations used to collect data. Most studies were restricted to relatively small samples. Most studies in this first category focused on the development of children, although some did include issues about parental functioning.

*Child development*
Studies investigating the development of children raised in lesbian families but born to the (lesbian) mother in a previous relationship mainly focus on sexual identity, emotional/behavioral development, social relationships and cognitive functioning of the children.
*Sexual identity.* Research on sexual identity focused on three important aspects, namely gender identity (self-identification as male or female), gender role behavior (preference for behaviors that are culturally associated with men or with women) and sexual orientation (attraction to and choice of sexual partners) (Money & Ehrhardt 1972).

In several small sample studies, these aspects of sexual identity were examined in children of lesbian mothers and compared with the sexual identity aspects of children of single heterosexual mothers. Gender identity was investigated using interviews, projective techniques (Golombok, Spencer, & Rutter, 1983), or standardized questionnaires in case of older children (Gottman & Sussman, 1990). None of these studies reported evidence were having difficulties with their gender identity. Gender role behavior was investigated by interviewing mothers and children about, for example, children's preferences for gender-typical activities. Green et al. (1986) reported no differences for boys on gender role behavior. However, more daughters of lesbian mothers than those of heterosexual mothers preferred masculine activities and more often showed a preference for masculine occupations. However, in other studies no differences between children in the two kinds of families were found on gender role behavior (Hoeffer, 1981; Kirkpatrick, Smith, & Roy, 1981; Hotveld & Mandel, 1982; Golombok, Spencer, & Rutter, 1983; Gottman & Sussman, 1990; Javaid, 1993). Hoeffer (1981) also examined lesbian and heterosexual mothers' toy preference for their children. Results revealed that lesbian mothers more frequently preferred a mixture of typical toys for boys and girls than did heterosexual mothers. In a study of divorced lesbian mothers and divorced gay fathers (Harris & Turner 1985), it was found that fathers were more likely to report encouraging sex-typed toy play in their children compared to mothers. Some studies also investigated the sexual orientation of adolescents and youngsters having a lesbian mother (Green, 1978; Golombok, Spencer, & Rutter, 1983; Huggins, 1989; Gottman & Sussman, 1990; Golombok & Tasker,1996; Tasker & Golombok, 1995; Tasker & Golombok, 1997). Although few children of lesbian mothers identified themselves as gay, lesbian or bisexual, the number of youngsters having a same-sex orientation did not differ from controls of youngsters having a heterosexual mother. However, it was also found that the children of lesbian mothers were more likely to consider the possibility of a same-sex relationship (Tasker & Golombok, 1995; Golombok & Tasker 1996; Tasker & Golombok, 1997).

*Emotional/behavioral development, and social relationships.* A variety of aspects of emotional and behavioral development of children from lesbian parents have been studied, such as their psychological adjustment (Tasker & Golombok, 1995; Tasker & Golombok, 1997) and self-concept (Huggins, 1989). It has been established that there are no differences between children of lesbian parents and those of heterosexual parents (Kirkpatrick, Smith, & Roy, 1981; Tasker & Golombok, 1995; Tasker & Golombok, 1997). In addition, it seems that children do not have emotional problems or react negatively when they become fully aware of their mother's sexual orientation (Stevens, Perry, Burston, Golombok, & Golding, 2003). A few studies also included aspects of children's peer relationships (Golombok, Spencer, & Rutter, 1983; Tasker & Golombok, 1995, 1997) and stigmatization (Green, 1978; Lewis, 1980; Tasker & Golombok, 1995). As with gender development and emotional and behavioral development, studies on social relationships revealed no differences between the children of lesbian parents and those of heterosexual parents (Golombok, Spencer, & Rutter, 1983; Gottman & Sussman, 1990; Tasker & Golombok, 1995; Tasker & Golombok, 1997). However, it was demonstrated that the children of lesbian mothers worried about the potential reactions of their peers (O' Connell, 1993; Tasker & Golombok, 1995), and minor incidents of teasing by peers were reported (Green, 1978; O' Connell, 1993; Tasker & Golombok, 1995). In the largest study to date on adolescent children of lesbian mothers (born in a previous heterosexual relationship), Gershon et al. (1999) examined the impact of societal factors on psychological well being. The study shows that adolescents who perceive more stigmatization have lower self-esteem.

*Cognitive functioning.* Two studies (Kirkpatrick, Smith, & Roy, 1981; Green,

**Table 2.1 Overview of empirical studies on lesbian families with children born in a previous heterosexual relationship**

| Authors | Main topics | Sample size | Age of children | Control group | Measures | Main results |
|---|---|---|---|---|---|---|
| Green, 1978 | Children's gender identity, gender role behavior, sexual orientation, stigmatization Marital attitudes | 21 children of non-single lesbian mothers | 5-14 | None | Structured interview, standardized tests | No atypical variation on gender identity, gender role behavior or sexual orientation Minor incidents of teasing |
| Mucklow & Phelan, 1979 | Self-concept of the mothers | 34 lesbian mothers | 6-9 | 47 heterosexual mothers | Standardized questionnaires | No differences between lesbian and heterosexual mothers on marital attitudes or self-concept |
| Lewis, 1980 | Stigmatization | 21 children of non-single lesbian mothers | 9-26 | None | Interviews | Children are worried about reactions from peers, however, no specific incidents were reported |
| Hoeffer, 1981 | Children's gender role behavior Mother's preference for gender-typed toys for their children | 20 single lesbian mothers and their children | | 20 single hetero-sexual mothers and their children | Structured Interview, standardized tests, standardized questionnaires | No differences between children in lesbian and those in heterosexual families on gender role behavior Lesbian mothers prefer more often a mixture of masculine and feminine toys for their children |
| Kirkpatrick, 1981 | Children's gender identity, gender role behavior, emotional functioning, cognitive functioning | 20 children of single lesbian mothers | 5-12 | 20 children of single hetero-sexual mothers | Semi-structured Interview, standardized tests | No differences between children in lesbian and those in heterosexual families on gender identity, gender role behavior, emotional functioning or cognitive functioning |
| Miller, Jacobsen, & Bigner, 1981 | Child-orientation of mothers | 34 lesbian mothers | | 47 heterosexual mothers | Standardized Questionnaires, inter-views | Lesbian mothers are more Child-oriented |

| Study | Variables | Sample | Age | Comparison group | Method | Findings |
|---|---|---|---|---|---|---|
| Hotveld & Mandel, 1982 | Children's gender identity, gender role behavior, cognitive functioning | 50 children of lesbian mothers | 3-11 | 35 children of heterosexual mothers | Standardized tests (child), interviews with mother and child | No differences between children in lesbian and heterosexual families on gender identity, gender role behavior or cognitive functioning |
| Lewin & Lyons, 1982 | Problems, experiences and support as coping strategy | 43 lesbian mothers | | 37 single heterosexual mothers | Interviews | Families of origin, more than lesbian networks, relied on for support |
| Rand, Graham, & Rawlings, 1982 | Mothers' psychological health | 25 lesbian mothers | | None | Standardized questionnaires, interviews | Psychological health of lesbian mothers within normal range |
| Golombok, Spencer, & Rutter, 1983 | Children's gender identity, gender role behavior, sexual orientation, behavioral adjustment, emotional functioning and peer relationship. Quality of parent-child relationship | 37 lesbian mothers (single & couples) and their children | 5-17 | 38 single heterosexual mothers | Structured interviews with mother and child separately, standardized questionnaires for mother and teacher (sexual orientation only for older children) | No differences between children in lesbian and those in heterosexual families on gender identity, gender role behavior, sexual orientation, peer relationship or quality of parent-child relationship. Higher incidence of psychiatric problems among children of single heterosexual mothers |
| Harris & Turner, 1985 | Children's gender role behavior | 10 gay fathers, 13 lesbian mothers, 2 heterosexual single fathers, and 14 heterosexual single mothers | 5-31 | | Standardized questionnaires | Gay fathers report more often that they encouraged gender-typed toy play in comparison to lesbian women |
| Green, Mandel, Hotveld, Gray, & Smith, 1986 | Children's gender identity, gender role behavior, emotional functioning and cognitive functioning | 56 children of lesbian mothers (single & couples) | 3-11 | 48 single heterosexual mothers | Standardized questionnaires, structured interviews, standardized tests | No differences between children in lesbian and those in heterosexual families on gender identity, and emotional and cognitive functioning. Girls in lesbian families more often prefer male-typed activities, clothes and occupations |

**Table 2.1 Overview of empirical studies on lesbian families with children born in a previous heterosexual relationship**

| Authors | Main topics | Sample size | Age of children | Control group | Measures | Main results |
|---|---|---|---|---|---|---|
| Huggins, 1989 | Children's self-concept and sexual orientation | 18 children of lesbian mothers | 13-19 | 18 children of heterosexual mothers | Standardized interviews and questionnaires | No differences between children in lesbian and heterosexual families on self-concept and sexual orientation |
| Levy, 1989 | Identity and social support | 31 lesbian mothers | 18-44 | None | Interviews & questionnaires | Lesbianism is a positive identity. Support received from friends rather than from extended family |
| Gottman & Sussman, 1990 | Children's gender Identity, gender role behavior, sexual orientation, and social adjustment | 33 children of lesbian mothers | | 33 children of heterosexual mothers | Standardized questionnaires | No differences between children of lesbian and of heterosexual mothers on gender identity, gender role behavior, sexual orientation and social adjustment |
| Koeple, Hare & Moran, 1992 | Couple relationship Satisfaction | 47 lesbian couples with children | | 32 lesbian couples without children | Standardized questionnaires | Couples with children scored higher on relationship satisfaction |
| Javaid, 1993 | Children's gender role behavior | 26 children of lesbian non-single mother | | 28 children of single heterosexual mothers | Interviews with children and mothers | No differences in gender role behavior |
| O'Connell, 1993 | Stigmatization | 11 children of lesbian mothers | | None | Interviews | Children are worried about reactions from peers. No specific incidents were reported |
| Lott-Whitehead & Tully, 1993 | Social networks and social support | 45 lesbian mothers | | None | Interviews, questionnaires | Lack of support from lesbian social networks. Families rely on social support from families of origin |
| Lewin, 1993 | Problems experiences And support as coping strategy | 73 lesbian mothers | 17-35 | 62 single heterosexual mothers | Interviews | Families of origin, more than lesbian networks, relied on for support |

| Reference | Focus | Sample | Age | Comparison group | Method | Results |
|---|---|---|---|---|---|---|
| Tasker & Golombok, 1995, 1997 (follow-up of Golombok, Spencer, & Rutter, 1983). Also published in: Golombok & Tasker, 1996 | Family relationships, peers, psychological adjustment, sexual Orientation, and Stigmatization | 25 children of lesbian mothers (single & non-single) | 17-35 | 21 children of heterosexual mothers (single & non-single) | Semi-structured interviews, standardized Questionnaires | No differences between children of lesbian and of heterosexual mothers on family relationships, peer relation, psychological adjustment and sexual orientation. A tendency for children with a lesbian mother to have been teased about their own sexual orientation. |
| Gershon, Tschann, & Jemerin, 1999 | Self-esteem, perceived stigmatization | 76 children of lesbian mothers | 11-18 | None | Standardized Questionnaires | Adolescents who experienced more stigmatization have lower self-esteem |
| Stevens, Perry, Burston, Golombok, & Golding, 2003 | How children deal towards others with sexual orientation of the mother openness | 38 lesbian mothers (28 born in a previous heterosexual relationship of the mother) | 5-9 | None | Standardized Interviews | Children are aware of mother's sexual orientation, they developed this awareness gradually and did not react negatively on this |

Mandel, Hotveld, Gray, & Smith, 1986) assessed children's cognitive functioning by using standardized tests. In these inquiries, no differences appeared between children in lesbian and those in heterosexual families on intelligence scales.

*Parental functioning*

Most studies on parental functioning in lesbian families with children born in a previous heterosexual relationship examined two aspects, namely the mother's psychological health and her parenting skills. In some small sample studies, other aspects were investigated, such as partner relationship satisfaction and social support.

*Mothers' psychological health.* A number of studies have compared the overall mental health of lesbian mothers with that of heterosexual mothers. The results show that there are no differences in psychological health between lesbian mothers and divorced heterosexual mothers in self-concept (Mucklow & Phelan, 1979; Rand, Graham, et al., 1982), happiness (Rand, Graham, & Rawlings, 1982) and overall adjustment and psychiatric status (Golombok, Spencer, & Rutter, 1983 ). Furthermore, Rand et al. (1982) showed that lesbian mothers who are open about their sexual orientation to their employer, ex-husband and children have fewer psychological health problems than do those who are not open about their sexual orientation or lifestyle.

*Maternal skills.* Miller, Jacobsen and Bigner (1981) investigated 34 lesbian and 47 heterosexual mothers, and reported that the former group was more child oriented in disciplinary techniques than the latter group was. Golombok et al. (1983) compared the quality of the parent-child relationship measured using a standardized interview. No differences were established between the lesbian and the heterosexual mothers.

*Other aspects.* Koeple, Hare and Moran (1992) compared relationship satisfaction of lesbian couples having children with those who not having children. It appeared that couples having children were more satisfied with their partner relationship than were couples without children. With respect to social support, Levy's study (1989) demonstrated that the 31 lesbian women interviewed especially received support from close networks of mostly lesbian friends. However, there have been conflicting findings on this matter. For example, it was found that families of origin are relied on more for support than lesbian networks are (Leurin & Lyons, 1982; Lewin, 1993), and many lesbian parents were disillusioned by the lack of support from and acceptance by lesbian social networks (Lott-Whitehead & Tully, 1993).

*Conclusion and limitations*

In general, no differences emerged on aspects of child development and parental functioning between families consisting of a divorced lesbian mother and those with a divorced heterosexual mother. The findings of these early inquiries cannot be generalized to lesbian families with children raised by the lesbian mother from the start. Firstly, lesbian families with children originating from a heterosexual relationship differ from planned lesbian families, because the parental composition has changed and both parent and child have experienced divorce and coming-out of the mother. In addition, most children in lesbian families who were born in a heterosexual couple lived with their father during the first years of life. Based on the assumption that early experiences may influence later development, these findings cannot be generalized to children born to lesbian couples.

### Studies on planned lesbian families

Twenty-one of the articles reviewed describe the results of studies on planned lesbian families (see Table 2.2). In these studies data were collected by means of interviews, self-administered questionnaires and standardized test as well. One study was based on observations. Most studies included a control group of heterosexual families. However, in several studies single – and two-mother lesbian families were collapsed. In some studies the control group consisted of heterosexual families with either conventionally conceived children or children conceived with artificial insemination with donor sperm (AID). Other studies combined both types of heterosexual families.

*Development of children*

Several studies examined topics related to the development of children, namely gender role behavior, emotional/social behavioral development, cognitive functioning, peer relationships, and stigmatization (e.g., being teased or bullied). In most studies more than one child outcome was examined. Furthermore, a Belgian follow-up study examined issues related to what children would like to know about their donor (Vanfraussen, Ponjaert-Kristoffersen, & Brcwacys, 2001).

*Gender role behavior*. Patterson (1994) examined gender role behavior of 37 children (aged 4 to 9) of lesbian mothers in an uncontrolled study using a standard child interview about preferences for gender role behavior (e.g., peer friendships, favorite toys, and games). She concluded that gender role preferences of children of lesbian mothers were within the expected range for children this age. In two other studies, gender role behavior was assessed using a validated questionnaire (Preschool Activity Inventory) filled out by the parents (Brewaeys, Ponjaert, Van Hall, & Golombok, 1997) or the children in a standard interview (Golombok et al., 2003). In neither study differences were reported between children in lesbian and children in heterosexual families. In one of the first inquiries on planned lesbian families, however, Steckel (1987) did find differences between children in both family types on gender role behavior. Steckel (1987) compared 11 preschool children of lesbian mothers with 11 same-age children of heterosexual couples, and found that the daughters of lesbian mothers tended to aspire non-traditional gender occupations more than the other children did.

*Emotional/social behavioral development*. Steckel (1987) also compared children of lesbian mothers with those of heterosexual couples on separation/individuation processes and aggression. Although no differences appeared between children in both kinds of families on separation/individuation, children of lesbian mothers

**Table 2.2 Overview of empirical studies on planned lesbian families**

| Authors | Main topics | Sample size | Age of children | Control group | Measures | Main results |
|---|---|---|---|---|---|---|
| McCandlish, 1987 | Children's gender identity, behavioral adjustment & parental role | 7 lesbian couples and their children | 2-7 | None | Structured interviews (mother and child) Observations of children during the interviews | No specific problems with respect to behavioral adjustment or gender identity Strong attachment between child and both parents |
| Steckel, 1987 | Separation/individuation process | 11 children of lesbian couples | 3-4 | 11 children of heterosexual couples | Structured interviews and questionnaires (mothers) Stancardized test (children) | No differences or difficulties in separation/individuation process |
| Brewaeys, Ponjaert, Van Steirteghem, & Devroey, 1993 | Attitudes parents towards donor insemination | 25 lesbian couples | 3 month – 7 years | 25 heterosexual couples (who have used AID) | Structured interviews | Heterosexual couples chose secrecy and saw AID as an opportunity to become a 'normal' family. Lesbian couples intended to inform their children. |
| Hare & Richards, 1993 | Social mother's parental responsibility and child's birth context (i.e. born during a previous heterosexual relationship or to the lesbian couple) | | | | Structured interviews | Partners in planned lesbian families took more responsibility |
| Patterson, 1994 | Children's gender role behavior, social competence, behavioral adjustment, and self-concept | 37 lesbian mothers (single & couples) and their children | 4-9 | None | Structured interviews (mothers) Standardized questionnaires | No differences with respect to norms. |
| Brewaeys, Devroey, Helmerhorst, Van Hall, & Ponjaert, 1995 | Opinions from lesbian mothers about donor anonymity | 50 lesbian couples | 1-2 | None | Standardized | Most couples were positive about donor identity registration |

| Study | Variables | Sample | Age | Comparison group | Method | Findings |
|---|---|---|---|---|---|---|
| Flaks, Ficher, Masterpasqua, & Joseph, 1995 | Children's behavioral adjustment, social competence and cognitive functioning, and parental skills | 15 lesbian couples and children | 3-8 | None | Standardized questionnaires for parent and teacher. Standardized test (child) | No differences between children in lesbian and those in heterosexual family. Lesbian parents more aware of parental skills |
| Patterson, 1995 | Division of labor and partner's relationship satisfaction | 26 lesbian couples | 4-9 | None | Standardized questionnaires | Biological mothers more involved in childcare; relationship satisfaction is high |
| Gartrell, Hamilton, Banks, Moshbacher, Reed, Sparks, & Bishop, 1996 | Transition to parenthood | 84 lesbian families (single & couples) | | None | Semi-structured interviews | Children are carefully planned and the decision to have children is made with support of close friends, networks and family |
| Sullivan, 1996 | Division of family tasks | 34 lesbian couples | | None | Interviews | Most families have a equitable practices with a equal sharing |
| Brewaeys, Ponjaert, Van Hall, & Golombok, 1997 | Children's gender role behavior and behavioral adjustment Quality of parent-child relationship Partner relationship satisfaction Paid employment | 30 lesbian couples | 4-8 | 52 heterosexual couples (26 AID and 26 children conventionally conceived) | Standardized questionnaires and standardized interviews | Greater mother-child interaction in lesbian families compared to single heterosexual mothers. No differences between groups on mother's psychological status and child outcomes |
| Golombok, Tasker, & Murray, 1997 | Quality of parent-child relationship, psychological status of mother, children's behavioral adjustment | 30 lesbian mother families (single & couples) | 3-9 | 42 single heterosexual mothers, 41 two-parent heterosexual families | Standardized questionnaires, structured interviews | Greater mother-child interaction in lesbian families compared to single heterosexual families. No differences on child outcomes or mental health status of mother |

**Table 2.2 Overview of empirical studies on planned lesbian families**

| Authors | Main topics | Sample size | Age of children | Control group | Measures | Main results |
|---|---|---|---|---|---|---|
| Chan, Brooks, Raboy & Patterson, 1998; | Division of family tasks Couples' relationship satis-faction | 30 lesbian couples | 5-? | 16 heterosexual couples (AID) | Standardized questionnaires | Lesbian biological and social mothers shared childcare tasks more equally than heterosexual parents did. Lesbian social mothers who are more satisfied with the division were also more satisfied with their relation-ships and reported fewer behavioral problems |
| Chan, Brooks, Raboy, & Patterson, 1998 | Behavioral adjustment, Parental stress | 55 lesbian mothers (single & couples) and their children | Mean: 7 | 25 heterosexual couples (single & couples) | Standardized questionnaires for parents and teachers | Children's behavioral adjustment was unrelated to parental sexual orientation or the number of parents |
| Gartrell, Banks, Reed, Hamilton, Rodas, & Deck, 1999 | Division of tasks Parent- child relationship | 156 lesbian mothers | | | Interviews | Most couples shared parenting equally |
| Patterson, 2001 | Maternal mental health, child's adjustment | 37 lesbian families (all couples) | 4-9 | No | Standardized questionnaires (mothers), structured interviews (child) | Assessment of children's adjustment were associated with measures of maternal health |
| Vanfraussen, Ponjaert-Kristoffersen, & Brewaeys, 2001 | Attitudes toward Donor anonymity | 41 children 45 lesbian parents (single and couples) | 7-17 | No | Interview | 46% of the children wanted to know more about the donor and 54% preferred donor anonymity |
| Morris, Balsam, & Rothblum, 2002 | Demographics, Mental health | 1,119 nonlesbian mothers, 187 lesbian mothers with children before coming out, 3131 with children after after coming out | | | Standardized Questionnaires | Lesbian mothers who gave birth before coming out have psychosocial health problems |

| Author, Year | Focus | Sample | Age | Comparison | Method | Findings |
|---|---|---|---|---|---|---|
| Vanfraussen, Ponjaert-Kristoffersen, &Brewaeys, 2002 | Children's psychological well being, and teasing | 24 children of lesbian families (single & couples) | 7 – 17 | 24 heterosexual families (children conventional conceived; single & couples) | Standardized questionnaires (children, parents and teacher), and structured interviews with children | Children share the fact that they live in a 2-mother family with close friends who react positively. For some peers it is hard to understand this family situation. Children of are more prone to family-related teasing incidents. No differences on child outcomes as reported by parents. Teachers indicate that children from lesbian families experience more attention problems |
| Golombok, Perry, Burston, Murray, Mooney-Somers, Stevens, & Golding, 2003 | Parent-child relationship, Parent's psychological status, Children's gender role behavior, psychological adjustment and peer relations | 39 lesbian mother families (20 single & 19 couples) | 5 – 10 | 134 heterosexual families (60 single mother families and 74 couples) | Standardized questionnaires (children and parents) and structured interviews | No differences between both families on child outcomes. Lesbian social mothers were less emotional involved with the children than fathers |
| Vanfraussen, Pontjaert-Kristoffersen, & Brewaeys, 2003 | Quality of parent-child relationship | 24 lesbian mother families (single & couples) | Mean: 10.4 | 24 heterosexual families (single & couples) | Standardized questionnaires and structured interviews with children | No differences in parent-child relationship between lesbian biological and social mother. Fathers are less involved in child activities than social mothers. |

were less likely to show aggressive behavior than children of heterosexual parents. Similar findings, based on interviews with seven lesbian mother families, were reported by McCandlish (1987). In several studies, results on emotional/social behavioral development were based on the Child Behavioral Checklist completed by mothers and teachers (McCandlish, 1987; Patterson, 1994; Brewaeys, Ponjaert, Van Hall, & Golombok, 1997). Chan et al. (1998), and Flaks et al. (1998) found no differences between children in lesbian and those in heterosexual families on emotional/social behavioral development, while Patterson (1994) demonstrated that children in lesbian families did not deviate from standards provided by the authors of the scale. Finally, Vanfraussen (2002) identified in a comparison of 24 planned lesbian families and 24 heterosexual families no differences on emotional/social development, as reported by the parents or the youngsters themselves. However, findings from the questionnaires filled in by their teachers indicated that the children in the former group display more attentional problems than do those in the latter group.

*Cognitive functioning.* Flaks et al. (1998) compared intelligence scores as measured by the WPPSI and the WISC-R, between children of lesbian couples and heterosexual couples. No differences were obtained.

*Peer relationships.* Vanfraussen et al. (2002) reported that children in lesbian families were not teased more frequently than children in heterosexual families on matters such as clothing and physical appearance. However, family-related teasing incidents were mentioned only by the children in lesbian families. It also appeared that children in lesbian families informed their peers spontaneously that they lived in a two-mother family. In general, close friends reacted positively. However, the children also reported that it was hard for some peers to understand that someone has two mothers without having a father. Similar findings were reported in the National Lesbian Family Study of Gartrell et al. (2000). Golombok et al. (2003) examined children's peer relationships in 39 lesbian and 134 heterosexual families. This study, were lesbian families were recruited through the Avon Longitudinal Study of Parents and Children (ALSPAC), was unique because findings on lesbian families were based on a non-convenience sample. Because extensive background information was available in the ALSPAC about household composition of the parents, it was possible to compare planned lesbian families with heterosexual families. No significant differences emerged between children in lesbian families and those in heterosexual families on perceptions of peer interactions.

*Donor information.* In a qualitative study Vanfraussen et al. (2001) found that all children of planned lesbian families involved in a longitudinal investigation at the Free University Hospital in Brussels, were aware that they had been conceived by means of donor insemination. Half of them were curious to find out more about the donor, although they did not consider him as part of the family. Half of the children preferred donor anonymity.

*Parental functioning*

The following topics with respect to parental functioning have been examined in studies of planned lesbian families: division of family tasks and employment, parental child rearing behavior (awareness of parental skills and quality of the parent-child relationship) and maternal psychological health. A few studies collected information about lesbian women's transition to parenthood and their opinion about using a sperm donor.

*Division of family tasks and employment.* Research on the division of family tasks shows that most lesbian couples with young children share child rearing (Sullivan, 1996; Gartrell et al., 2000 ), to a greater degree than heterosexual couples do (Patterson 1994; Brewaeys, Ponjaert, Van Hall, & Golombok, 1997; Flaks, Ficher, Masterpasqua, & Joseph, 1995). Although lesbian parents share child rearing more equally than heterosexual parents, no differences emerged between lesbian and heterosexual parents on satisfaction with involvement in family tasks (Chan, Brooks, Raboy, & Patterson, 1998). In these studies, division of time was measured primarily by means of questionnaires, that is, retrospectively. The questionnaires asked respondents to rate the distribution of time over several tasks.

*Parental child rearing behavior.* Only a few studies focused on parental child rearing behavior. McCandlish (1987) reported in a study of seven lesbian families that both the biological and the social mother developed a strong attachment to the child. Other studies found indications that the non-biological mothers (the social mothers) in planned lesbian families demonstrated a higher quality of parent-child interaction (Brewaeys, Ponjaert, Van Hall, & Golombok, 1997; Flaks, Ficher, Masterpasqua, & Joseph, 1995; Golombok, Tasker, & Murray, 1997) and parenting awareness skills (Flaks, Ficher, Masterpasqua, & Joseph, 1995) than do fathers in heterosexual families. In addition, in most studies it was observed that lesbian partners in the two-mother families experienced a higher level of synchronicity in parenting than did heterosexual partners. Thus in heterosexual families, mothers scored significantly higher than fathers on, for example, the quality of parent-child interaction, while within the lesbian families no differences emerged between the two parents. Vanfraussen et al. (2003) showed that the quality of the parent-child relationship experienced by the social mother is comparable to that of the biological mother. Unlike fathers in heterosexual families, the lesbian social mother is equally involved in child activities as the lesbian biological mother is. These findings were based on parental self-reports from 24 lesbian families and 24 heterosexual families. In this study, the children were also interviewed about the parent-child relationship. Children in lesbian families experienced as much acceptance and authority from both parents as children in heterosexual families. Golombok and colleagues (2003), however, found in the ALSPAC study that social mothers were less likely to show raised levels of emotional involvement with their children than fathers in heterosexual families. It should be mentioned that, although the children involved in this study were born to a lesbian couple, a large percentage of the lesbian social mothers were stepmothers. Hare and Richards (1993) compared the parental role of social mothers in planned lesbian families with that of social mothers in lesbian families whose children were born in a heterosexual relationship. It turned out that social mothers in planned lesbian families took more parental responsibility.

*Mothers' psychological health.* No differences were found between the psychological health of lesbian mothers and that of heterosexual mothers (Golombok et al., 2003). Patterson (2001) reported in study of 37 lesbian families that lesbian mothers who described their own psychological adjustment and self-esteem in positive terms were more likely to report that their children were developing well. Morris, Balsam and Rothblum (2002) found that lesbians who gave birth to children before coming out were more likely to have had mental health counseling than were those who gave birth to children after coming out.

*Transition to parenthood.* Gartell et al. (1996) collected descriptive information about 84 lesbian families. Their findings, which are based on interviews with mothers, show that children are highly desired and carefully planned. The women in this study made their decisions with the help of close friendship networks.

*Opinion about donor insemination.* Brewaeys et al. (1993) interviewed 25 lesbian and 25 heterosexual parents who used an anonymous sperm donor. The interviews revealed different attitudes concerning the use of donor insemination. Heterosexual parents saw AID as an opportunity to become a 'normal' family, and most of them had decided not to tell their children or other people about the use of a donor. The lesbian parents, however, intended to inform their children that they had used a donor. In another study, Brewaeys et al. (1995) investigated the opinion of lesbian mothers about the desirability of knowing the identity of the donor: 56% were positive about identity registration.

## Conclusion and limitations

Investigations in which planned lesbian families were compared with heterosexual families revealed no differences in child outcomes such as behavioral adjustment and gender identity. It is remarkable that the studies that also examined parental behavior indicated that the parent-child relationship in planned lesbian families is better than it is in heterosexual families. However, positive or negative consequences in psychological development of the child have not yet been established. It may be that increasing levels of warmth and parental involvement do not result in increasing levels of child well being once a certain threshold is passed (Roberts, 1986; Roberts & Strayer, 1987).

On the other hand, the studies reviewed have shortcomings. For example, they did not take into account the divergent division of family tasks in planned lesbian families, or other aspects where lesbian families and heterosexual families might differ, such as desire to have children and division of tasks.

Furthermore, most of the studies had relatively small samples and most data consisted of self-reports (questionnaires or standardized interviews) by the parents. Another limitation is that in several studies, the sample comprised both single – and two-mother lesbian families. The control group of heterosexual parents was also diverse. In some studies, children in lesbian families were compared with children in heterosexual families who had been conceived in a conventional way, while in other studies a comparison was made/also made with children in heterosexual families who had been conceived through donor insemination.

To date, researchers have only examined child development and parental functioning. They have not studied internal family processes – such as parenthood motives and desire, and parental experiences of parenthood and child rearing goals – or external relationships, such as the social support of these families in comparison to heterosexual families. Existing research considers planned lesbian families primarily as a homogenous group, rather than as a heterogeneous group with respect to, for example, experiences with negative attitudes towards their non-traditional family situation.

## 2.4 Discussion

Research on lesbian families only started about 25 years ago and proceeded two phases. To begin with, systematic studies of lesbian families focused on lesbian families with children who were born to the mother in a previous heterosexual relationship. Much of this early research was designed to evaluate judicial presumptions about the negative consequences for the psychological health and well being of the children in these families. More recently, however, studies included lesbian families whose children were born to the lesbian couple (planned lesbian families).

Studies in both phases have emphasized that lesbian and heterosexual families are very much alike and that children in both family types are 'impossible to (be) distinguished' (Chan, Raboy, & Patterson, 1998, p. 453). Studies in the first phase were used to support lesbian parents in custody cases, and those in the second phase to support lesbian women who were fighting for equal rights to adopt children or for access to donor insemination services (Harne, 1997; Clarke, 2002). By emphasizing the similarity between lesbian and heterosexual families, research has failed to show processes in which lesbian and heterosexual families differ, for instance their desire and motivation to have children. Lesbian families and heterosexual families may differ in this respect because of their special circumstances. For lesbian women, for example, impregnation is a more complex process than it is for fertile heterosexual couples. Lesbian families and heterosexual families may also differ in experiences of parenthood and non-traditional child rearing goals. As result of being a lesbian parent in a society with less favorable attitudes towards lesbian parenting. Studying aspects in the family processes where lesbian and heterosexual families diverge would be a challenge for future research. The next step would be to investigate whether these differences in family functioning also result in differences in the parent-child relationship. Although family functioning in lesbian families might be just as varied, challenging, comforting, amusing and frustrating as it is in heterosexual families, it is the stigma of lesbianism and the lack of acknowledgement of lesbianism that makes their family life different (Nelson, 1996). Further examination of the stigmatization of these families would be another challenge for future research on planned lesbian families.

Research on lesbian families is of interest in its own right, and it is important to include studies on lesbian women in mainstream research (Herek, Kimmel, Amaro, & Melton, 1991; More & Rochlen, 1999). However, research in the field of planned lesbian families may also lead to a better understanding of family processes and of the development of children in 'normal' families as well.

## 2.5 Practical implications

Although lesbian families are non-traditional in structure, they are confronted with the same dilemmas as heterosexual families are. In addition, lesbian families are also confronted with issues that do not appear in the family situation of heterosexual families, including the decision to parent, pathways to parenthood, and societal homophobia. While some lesbians and their children might seek counseling services with issues and circumstances unrelated to their non-traditional family situation, for some lesbians these issues and circumstances may well be related to their unique family situation. It would therefore be erroneous for healthcare workers to overlook issues that are related to the non-traditional family situation of lesbian families. However, it would be equally erroneous to minimize the potential impact of stigmatization and homophobia on the family's experiences. Further research on this aspect is needed.

# III

# Planned lesbian families:
# Their desire and motivation to have children*

*The aim of this study was to examine whether planned lesbian families differ from heterosexual families on the desire and motivation to have a child. Hundred lesbian two-mother families were compared with 100 heterosexual families. Data were collected by means of questionnaires. Lesbian parents and heterosexual parents rank their parenthood motives rather similarly, however, happiness is significantly more important for lesbian mothers than it is for heterosexual parents, while identity development is less important for lesbian mothers than it is for heterosexual parents. Furthermore, compared to heterosexual parents, lesbian parents spend more time thinking about their motives for having children, and their desire to have a child is stronger.*

## 3.1  Introduction

The increased access to donor insemination since the 1980s has resulted in what several authors called a baby boom among lesbians (Morningstar, 1999; Patterson, 1995b; Weston, 1991). Regardless of this lesbian baby boom, there is a lack of knowledge about the motives behind the desire of lesbian women to procreate. In the present study, parenthood motives and the desire to have children were investigated among a large group of lesbian families.

In the literature two- mother families in which the child was born to the lesbian relationship are characterized as 'planned lesbian mother families' (Flaks, Ficher, Masterpasqua, & Joseph, 1995, p 105). In this relatively new family type, the two lesbian mothers (the biological mother and the social mother) plan having children together. This in contrast to lesbian families were children were born in a previous heterosexual relationship. In the Netherlands, were this study was carried out, among heterosexual families almost every baby is 'planned' as well, or at least not born unwanted. Fertility behavior in the Netherlands is well regulated, unwanted pregnancies are rare, and contraception is widely available and its use widespread (Latten & Cuijvers, 1994; Bonsel & Van Der Maas, 1994).

It is difficult to say how many lesbian parents there are (Patterson & Friel, 2000). In most Western industrialized countries the total number of lesbians who have given birth to a child within a lesbian relationship amounts to several thou-

* This chapter is based on: Bos, H.M.W., Van Balen, F & Van Den Boom, D.C. (2003). Planned lesbian families: Their desire and motivation to have children. *Human Reproduction*, 18, 2216-2224.

sands. Nevertheless this is an estimate. Probably, the majority of parents in planned lesbian families became pregnant through donor insemination (Patterson & Chan, 1999). Lesbian women, for example, can be impregnated at a fertility-clinic using sperm from a donor. In the Netherlands almost all fertility-clinics offer insemination services or IVF to unmarried women, including lesbians. There are, however, some Dutch clinics that refuse to provide such a service to lesbians or single parents (Commissie Gelijke Behandeling/ Equal Treatment Committee, 2000; de Graaf & Sandfort, 2000). Other lesbian couples opt for self-insemination using sperm provided by a male friend or relative. The present investigation is unique in that it focuses on a large group of planned lesbian families, consisting of lesbian couples who attended a fertility-clinic in order to become pregnant as well as lesbian couples who opted for self-insemination.

There is a body of literature presenting speculations about the motives behind human procreation in heterosexual relationships. Some authors attach great value to biological drives (Benedek, 1970a, 1970b). From a psychoanalytic perspective, motherhood is viewed as essential for women in order to develop a female identity. From a feminist perspective, however, the desire to have a child has been considered to be a consequence of social enforcement, and motherhood has often been criticized as a barrier to personal development and freedom (see for an overview: Thompson, 2002). Early feminist critics also associated new reproductive technologies with the glorification of traditional motherhood (Rowland, 1984; Hammer, 1984; Corea, 1985). Others, however, saw these technologies as a means to facilitate lesbian parenting and to break down compulsory heterosexuality (Arditti, Klein, & Minden, 1989).

Traditional research into the motives for wanting children has been centered on the cost and benefit model (Fawcett, 1972, 1978; Fawcett, Albores, & Arnold, 1972; Hoffman, 1972; Hoffman & Hoffman, 1973; Seccombe, 1991). Basic to this model is that people decide to have a child, or a second child, after consider the pros and cons of having children. Perceived costs seldom determine a woman from wanting a first child (Knijn, 1986; Van Balen & Trimbos-Kemper, 1995), but might be an important factor in the decision about the upper limit of the number of children she wants to have (Hoffman & Manis, 1979). Therefore, it is important to study parenthood motives from the perspective of why couples wish to become parents (Van Balen & Trimbos-Kemper, 1995). In recent years a number of studies have been carried out from this perspective. Of particular interest are studies of couples that become parents after assisted reproduction (Colpin, de Munter, & Vandemeulebroecke, 1998; Van Balen & Trimbos-Kemper, 1995; Langdridge, Connolly, & Sheeran, 2000). The underlying reason for studying parenthood motivation and the strength of the desire to have children is that these aspects are supposed to effect parenting and the parent-child relationship (Levy, 1970). Although lesbian mothers also have the experience of assisted reproduction, parenthood motives and desire have been addressed only sporadically among lesbian mothers. The purpose of the present research was to expand the knowledge about parenthood motivation in planned lesbian families. The present study is exceptional because it examines reasons for parenthood among a large group of planned lesbian families in comparison with those of heterosexual families. In order to decrease the possible confounding aspects of infertility a comparison was made with heterosexual families having naturally conceived children.

In the transition to parenthood, lesbian women are confronted with questions – sometimes critical ones – posed by their family, friends and other people in their environment (e.g., colleagues) about their motivation to have a child. Lesbian women are therefore forced to reflect on their desire to have children and to think, and rethink, their motives for wanting children more often than fertile heterosexual parents. Lesbian women who opt for donor spermatozoa in a hospital have to undergo an extensive intake interview with a counselor focused on their reasons for wanting to become a parent. In this respect, lesbian women are in a situation comparable to that of infertile heterosexual couples, who also have to explain their decision to family, friends and counselors. One would thus expect that lesbian couples, like infertile couples, spend more time reflecting on their desire to have a child than fertile heterosexual couples do.

Another aspect of the transition to parenthood is the strength of the desire to have children. Until recently, the intensity is of the desire to have children among lesbian couples has not been investigated and also not this desire is compared to fertile heterosexual couples. It is assumed that lesbian couples go to great lengths to pursue their desire to have a child, and that this desire is very strong among lesbian women. For most lesbian women, becoming pregnant is more complex than it is for fertile heterosexual couples, because lesbian women cannot become pregnant by having sex with their partner. For lesbians who want to become pregnant through self-insemination, it usually turns out not to be easy to find a sperm donor. In addition, lesbians who have decided to go to a fertility-clinic are often put on a waiting list. Due to these circumstances the intensity of the wish for a child is probably stronger among lesbian parents compared to heterosexual parents.

In sum, the aim of this study is to investigate the motives behind parenthood, the reflection involved in the desire to have a child, and the strength of this desire in lesbian parents, and to compare these aspects with heterosexual parents without history of fertility problems. In addition, the study examined the relation between reflection, the strength of the desire and the motives for having children.

## 3.2  Method

The study reported in this article investigates the desire and motivation of planned lesbian families to have children, and compares these aspects with those of a group of heterosexual families without history of fertility problems (e.g., heterosexual families having naturally conceived children). Both the lesbian and the heterosexual families were pre selected in being Dutch, because the questionnaire was in Dutch and in order to eliminate possible confounding effects of ethnic background.

*Recruitment and responses*

The planned lesbian family group was recruited through several entries: a medical centre for artificial insemination (response rate: 41.9%; N=18 couples), a mailing list for gay and lesbian parents (response rate: 78.3%; N=47 couples), and with the help of individuals with expertise in the area of gay and lesbian parenting (response rate: 45.3%; N=34 couples). Also, an advertisement was placed in a lesbian magazine. One family responded to the advertisement.

Some respondents of the group of heterosexual families were drawn from the population register of two cities. Others were contacted through schools and by means of referrals from participants in the lesbian family group. The total response rate was 21.4% (population register offices: 17.3%; professional contacts: 24.1% and referrals: 38.7%). Using this procedure we obtained a pool of 251 heterosexual families. From this pool, 100 families were selected to match with the lesbian-mother families on, for example, urbanization (population registration offices: 42 families; professional contacts: 49 families and referrals: 9 families).

Differences were found between the overall response rate among the lesbian family group and among the heterosexual family group, that is, 55.6% and 21.4% respectively. Based on the findings of previous research (Brewaeys, Ponjaert-Kristoffersen, Van Steirteghem, & Devroey, 1993; Jacob, Klock, & Maier, 1999; Wendland, Byrn, & Hill, 1996) we also expected that the response rate among lesbian families would be higher than among heterosexual families. The relatively high response rate in the lesbian family group may be associated with interest among lesbian couples on the topic of this study. For lesbian couples recruited through the fertility-clinic perhaps a feeling of obligation to do something in return for the medical assistance they had received, may have been an important reason to participate in the study. The response rate among heterosexual families was low, however, compared to the response rate in other Dutch studies on family issues (Brinkman, 2000; De Leeuw & De Heer, 2002).

*Measures*

Data concerning parenthood motivations, the time parents had spent thinking about the reasons for having children (reflection) and the desire to have a child (strength of the desire) were collected by means of a questionnaire. The instruments in this study were already used in previous research on parenthood motives among involuntary childless couples (Van Balen & Trimbos-Kemper, 1995), in research comparing IVF mothers with mothers conceiving children traditionally (Colpin, De Munter, & Vandemeulebroecke, 1998), and in research among female childless university students (Gerson, 1983). All questions about parenthood motives, reflection on and the strength of the desire to have a child targeted to the first child.

*Parenthood motives.* The Parenthood Motivation List (Van Balen & Trimbos-Kemper, 1995) was used to measure the motives for having a child. Six motives were distinguished in this self-report questionnaire: (1) happiness, (2) motherhood/ fatherhood, (3) well being, (4) identity, (5) continuity and, (6) social control. Happiness refers to expected feelings of affection and happiness in the relationship with children (e.g., 'Children make me happy'). Motherhood/fatherhood refers to the expectation that parenthood will provide life-fulfillment (e.g., 'Experience pregnancy/birth'). Well being refers to the expected positive effects on the family-relationship (e.g., 'Makes life complete'). Identity refers to the desire to have children as a means of achieving adulthood and identity strengthening (e.g., 'Sign of being grown up'). Continuity refers to the desired affective relationship with grown-up children and the wish to live on after death through one's children (e.g., 'To continue living'). Social control refers to implicit or explicit pressure from outside the couple to procreate (e.g., 'Is expected by others'). Each dimension consisted of three items and respondents were asked to rate the importance of each item at the moment they first thought about realizing their desire to have children. Responses were rated on a three-point scale (1=not important-3=very important). In the present study Cronbach's alpha for happiness, motherhood/ fatherhood, and well being were good ($\alpha$ = .62, .60, .65, respectively). Cronbach alpha's on identity, continuity, and social control were sufficient ($\alpha$ =. 52, .50, .50, respectively).

*Reflection.* To measure the reflection involved in the process of deciding to have children, we inquired about the time parents spent thinking about the reasons for having children (1=never-3=often).

*Strength of the desire to have children.* The strength of parent's desire to have children (intensity of desire) was assessed on a six-point Likert-scale. The following question was posed: 'what were you willing to give up in order to have children?' (1=it didn't really matter to me-6= more than anything). The respondents were also asked to compare the strength of their desire to have children with the strength of their partner's desire.

## Subjects

A total of 100 lesbian mother families and 100 heterosexual families without a history of fertility problems participated in this study. Because all questions about parenthood motives, reflection and the strength of the desire to have a child targeted the first child, we defined the biological mother in the lesbian family as the lesbian biological mother, and the other mother as the lesbian social mother. Only a minority (33%) of the social mothers of the first child later gave birth to another child. The majority of the lesbian couples (58) visited a fertility-clinic and used sperm from an anonymous (45) or identifiable donor (13). Nearly half of the lesbian couples (42) chose self-insemination.

Most families in our study, both lesbian-mother and heterosexual-parent families, lived in an (sub)urban area (91% and 94%, respectively). Mean age of the lesbian biological mothers at the time the first child was born was significantly higher than that of the heterosexual mothers (lesbian mothers: *M*= 34.6 years, *SD*= 3.32; heterosexual mothers: *M*= 31.6 years, *SD*= 3.84; *p* < .001). The lesbian social mothers' mean age at the time of birth of the first child was significantly higher than that of the heterosexual fathers (lesbian mothers: *M*=35.4 years, *SD*= 6.03; heterosexual fathers: *M*= 33.3 years, *SD*= 3.85; *p* < .01).

No significant difference emerged between the two family types on educational level and mean duration of the relationship. In both groups, most parents (75.5 %) had higher professional or academic schooling. The mean duration of the couples' relationship was 14.9 years for the lesbian couples (*SD*= 3.87), and 14.8 years (*SD*– 4.89) for the heterosexual couples.

*Statistical analysis*

To test for differences between lesbian and heterosexual parents on the transition to parenthood, multivariate analyses of variance (MANOVAs) were performed with parenthood motives, reflection and desire as the dependent variables, and family type as the independent variable. When Wilks' criterion was significant, a series of one-way ANOVAs was carried out. In order to compare lesbian biological mothers with heterosexual mothers, and lesbian social mothers with heterosexual fathers.

Demographic information about the sample showed that lesbian and heterosexual families differed in parental age at the time the first child was born. Therefore, when one-way ANOVAs showed a significant difference between lesbian biological mothers and heterosexual mothers, or between lesbian social mothers and heterosexual fathers, the initial group comparison was followed by an analysis of covariance using parental age at the time the first child was born, as the covariate.

To assess the relations between reflection, strength of desire and motives for having children, Pearson correlations were computed between variables examined, separately for lesbian mothers (both biological and social) and heterosexual parents (both fathers and mothers).

## 3.3   Results

*Parenthood motives, reflection and desire*

Multivariate analysis of variance was performed to establish significant differences between the lesbian families and the heterosexual families on parenthood motives, reflection and intensity of the desire to have children. Results using Wilks' criterion showed a significant effect, *F* (8, 384)= 18.21, *p* < .001. Table 3.1 presents the means and the standard deviations for lesbian biological and lesbian social mothers, and heterosexual mothers and fathers on all the variables assessed, as well as the results of univariate analyses of variance between lesbian biological and heterosexual mothers, and between lesbian social mothers and heterosexual fathers.

*Parenthood motives.* As presented before, six categories of motivation were discerned: happiness, well being, parenthood, identity, continuity and social control. As shown in Table 3.1, the order of the motives is quite similar for lesbian and heterosexual parents. The overall scores on such motives as happiness and parenthood are relatively high, whereas they are relatively low on social control.

Univariate analyses of variance between lesbian biological and heterosexual mothers on parenthood motives revealed significant differences on two scales (see Table 3.1). Happiness was significantly more important for lesbian biological mothers than for heterosexual mothers, and identity development was a significantly more important motive for heterosexual mothers than it was for lesbian biological mothers. For happiness and identity development the differences between biological and heterosexual mothers remained significant after controlling for parental age at the time of birth of the first child (happiness: $F$ (1, 197)= 4.98, $p < .05$; identity development: $F$ (1, 197)= 6.40, $p < .01$). No significant differences between lesbian biological and heterosexual mothers were established either for parenthood motive or for well being, continuity and social control.

No significant differences were emerged between lesbian social mothers and heterosexual fathers on parenthood motive. On the other hand, both groups differ significantly on the motives happiness, well being, continuity, identity development and social control (see Table 3.1). For lesbian social mothers, happiness was a significantly more important motive than it was for fathers. Nevertheless, well being, continuity, identity development, and social control were less important motives for lesbian social mothers than they were for fathers. Differences remained significant after controlling for age of the parent at the time of the birth of the first child (happiness: $F$ (1, 195)= 16.21, $p < .001$; well being: $F$ (1, 195)= 5.33, $p < .05$; continuity: $F$ (1, 194)= 4.93, $p < .01$; identity development: $F$ (1, 195)= 8.92, $p < .001$; social control: $F$ (1, 194)= 5.51, $p < .01$).

Within lesbian families, biological mothers differ significantly from social mothers on the motives happiness, parenthood and continuity: these motives were more important for the former than for the latter group (happiness; t= 2.11, df= 99, $p < .05$; parenthood: t= 3.66, df= 98, $p < .001$; continuity: t= 2.91, df= 98, $p < .01$). Being social mother of a first child does not imply that this mother cannot be the biological mother from later children. Compared to those social mothers who did not become a biological mother, parenthood and continuity were significantly more important for those social mothers who gave birth to a second or third child (parenthood: $M$= 2.50, $SD$= .51 versus $M$= 1.98, $SD$= .56, $p < .001$ and continuity: $M$= 1.44, $SD$= .38 versus $M$= 1.27, $SD$= .34, $p < .05$).Mothers in heterosexual families differ significantly from fathers, that is, for mothers happiness and parenthood are more important than for fathers (happiness: t= 2.94, df= 98, $p < .01$; parenthood: t= 3.81, df= 98, $p < .001$).

*Reflection.* Univariate analyses of variance between lesbian biological and heterosexual mothers, and between lesbian social mothers and heterosexual fathers, on time spent thinking about the reasons for having children (reflection) revealed significant differences (see Table 3.1). Lesbian biological and lesbian social mothers spent significantly more time on reflection than heterosexual mothers and heterosexual fathers, respectively. After controlling for parental age (at the time the first child was born) differences remained significant for both the former and the latter comparison, $F (1, 197)= 24.27$, $p < .001$ and $F (1, 195)= 25.59$, $p < .001$, respectively.

It was also examined whether parents within lesbian families, and within heterosexual families, differed on reflection. Within lesbian families, biological mothers of the first child spent significantly more time thinking about the reasons for wanting children than their partners ($t= 2.21$, $df= 97$, $p < .05$). In heterosexual families mothers and fathers did not differ significantly on this aspect. On reflection, social mothers in lesbian families who later became pregnant did not differ significantly from those mothers who did not become a biological mother.

*Strength of the desire to have children.* With respect to the strength of the desire to have children, lesbian biological mothers differ significantly from heterosexual mothers (see Table 3.1). The mean score of the lesbian biological mothers on the six-point Likert scale measuring strength of the desire was significantly higher than the mean score of heterosexual mothers. This effect remained significant after controlling for the parental age, $F (1, 197)= 26.35$, $p < .001$.

It was also found that lesbian social mothers and heterosexual fathers differ significantly on the intensity of the desire to have a child (see Table 3.1). Compared to heterosexual fathers lesbian social mothers mean score on desire was significantly higher. Differences remained significant after controlling for age of parent at the time the first child was born, $F (1, 193)= 6.05$, $p < .05$.

Furthermore, within lesbian families the strength of the desire to have children was significantly higher for the biological mother than it was for the social mother ($t=2.11$, $df= 99$, $p < .05$). On strength of desire, social mothers in lesbian families who later became pregnant did not differ significantly from those mothers who did not become a biological mother. Within heterosexual families, parents did not differ on desire. The strength of the desire to have children among mothers in heterosexual families was not significantly higher than among fathers in heterosexual families.

**Table 3.1 Parenthood motives (means and standard deviations) for lesbian and heterosexual parents**

| | Lesbian biological mothers | Heterosexual mothers | Lesbian social mothers | Heterosexual fathers | Lesbian biological mothers versus heterosexual mothers F-value | Lesbian social mothers versus heterosexual fathers F-value |
|---|---|---|---|---|---|---|
| *Parenthood motives* | | | | | | |
| Happiness | 2.75 (.33) | 2.60 (.46) | 2.66 (.44) | 2.40 (.48) | 7.15** | 15.88*** |
| Parenthood | 2.41 (.45) | 2.33 (.55) | 2.15 (.59) | 2.07 (.53) | 1.37 | 1.56 |
| Well being | 1.98 (.48) | 2.02 (.58) | 1.86 (.52) | 2.08 (.61) | .18 | 7.65** |
| Continuity | 1.46 (.40) | 1.53 (.45) | 1.33 (.36) | 1.48 (.44) | 1.16 | 6.76** |
| Identity | 1.24 (.34) | 1.42 (.45) | 1.26 (.40) | 1.47 (.47) | 10.38*** | 11.55** |
| Social Control | 1.10 (.22) | 1.12 (.20) | 1.07 (.20) | 1.15 (.29) | .37 | 6.05** |
| *Reflection* | 2.42 (.61) | 1.93 (.54) | 2.25 (.59) | 1.87 (.51) | 36.64*** | 23.60 |
| *Intensity desire* | 4.59 (.88) | 3.85 (1.18) | 4.27 (1.10) | 3.57 (1.06) | 25.22*** | 20.49*** |

*p<.05;  **p<.01;  ***p<.001

Lesbian biological mothers and lesbian social mothers did not significantly differ from mothers and fathers in heterosexual families with respect to how respondents compared their own desire to that of their partner (see Figure 3.1).

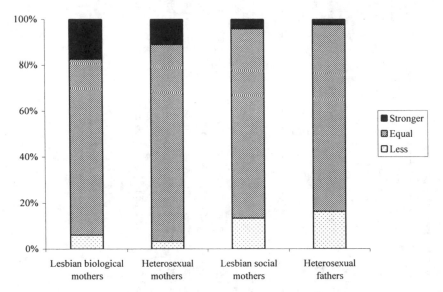

*Figure 3.1*    Perception of one's own desire to have a child
compared with partner's desire

However, there were significant differences between biological and social mothers in lesbian families, as well as between mothers and fathers in heterosexual families. Nineteen percent of the lesbian biological mothers experience their own desire to have children as being stronger than their partners' desire compared to 2.1% of the lesbian social mothers. Only 3.1% of the biological mothers in lesbian families versus 16.5% of the social mothers perceive their own desire as being weaker, $\chi^2$ (2, N= 195)= 22.71, $p < .001$. Among social mothers of the first child, there were no significant differences in this respect between those mothers who are and those who are not the biological mother of subsequent children.

In heterosexual families, more mothers than fathers experience their own desire as being stronger than that of their partner (11.0% as opposed to 2.3%), and 3.3% of the mothers and 16.3% of the fathers reported their own desire as being weaker than that of their spouse, $\chi^2$ (1, N= 177)= 12.75, $p < .01$.

Also, mutual assessment of the desire to have a child was analyzed. In 84.5% of the lesbian families and 79.3% of the heterosexual families there is a similarity between perceptions of the strength to have a child between both partners.

*Relation between reflection, the strength of the desire and motives*

*Reflection and strength of desire.* For lesbian parents (biological and social mothers), an intense desire to have children correlated with a high level of reflection (biological mothers: $r = .27$, $p < .01$; social mothers: $r = .32$, $p < .001$). Among heterosexual parents (mothers and fathers) no significant correlation between reflection and strength of desire was found.

*Motives and reflection.* Table 3.2 shows correlations between parenthood motives and reflection, for lesbian mothers (biological and social) and for heterosexual parents (mothers and fathers). For lesbian mothers (biological and social), the most important parenthood motives were significantly correlated with reflection. The more important the motives of happiness and parenthood, the more time they spent thinking about the reasons for having children. For lesbian biological mothers, well being was also significantly correlated with reflection. The more important this motive, the more time lesbian biological mothers spent on reflecting about having children. In addition, for lesbian mothers (biological and social) no significant correlation was found between the less important motives (identity development, continuity and social control) and reflection.

For the parents in the comparison group of heterosexual families, the motives happiness, parenthood, well being, identity and continuity did not correlate significantly with reflection. However, social control – the least important motive – did correlate significantly. The more important the motive of social control, the more time heterosexual parents (mothers and fathers) spent thinking about the reasons for wanting children.

*Motives and strength of desire.* Table 3.2 also shows the correlation between parenthood motives and the strength of the desire to have a child. For lesbian biological mothers, strength of this desire correlated significantly with the motive of parenthood. The more important this motive, the stronger the desire to have children. For lesbian biological mothers, no significant correlations were obtained between strength of desire and any of the other five motives. For lesbian social mothers and for fathers in heterosexual families, strength of desire was significantly correlated with the motives of happiness, parenthood and well being – the three most important motives for this group. The more important these motives were for lesbian social mothers and heterosexual fathers, the stronger the desire to have a child. Among mothers in the heterosexual comparison group it appeared that only identity development was not significantly correlated with the desire to have children. However, the more value these mothers attached to such motives as happiness, motherhood, well being, continuity and social control, the stronger the intensity of the desire to have children.

**Table 3.2 Pearson correlation coefficients between parenthood motives and reflection and strength of desire for children, for lesbian and heterosexual parents**

| | Reflection | | | | Strength of desire | | | |
|---|---|---|---|---|---|---|---|---|
| | Lesbian families | | Heterosexual families | | Lesbian families | | Heterosexual families | |
| | Biological mothers first child | Social mothers first child | Mothers | Fathers | Biological mothers first child | Social mothers first child | Mothers | Fathers |
| Happiness | .30** | .26* | .06 | .04 | .05 | .38*** | .22* | .39*** |
| Parenthood | .29** | .24* | .06 | .01 | .31** | .41*** | .28** | .20* |
| Well being | .28** | .16 | .13 | .07 | .04 | .21* | .23* | .36*** |
| Continuity | .17 | .10 | .04 | .13 | .10 | .01 | .20* | .15 |
| Identity | .18 | .09 | .03 | .05 | .10 | .09 | .12 | -.02 |
| Social Control | .01 | .11 | .21* | .21* | -.06 | -.13 | .33*** | .03 |

*$p$<.05; **$p$<.01; ***$p$<.001

## 3.4 Discussion

The aim of this study was to examine differences between lesbian mothers families and heterosexual families in the process of transition to parenthood. Hundred planned lesbian families and 100 heterosexual families were compared on several aspects of the decision-making process related to parenthood.

Before discussing and interpreting the results, it should be mentioned that educational level of the planned lesbian families involved in this study is high. Several studies have shown that lesbian women tend to be more highly educated (Steckel, 1987; McCandlish, 1987; Patterson, 1994; Flaks, Ficher, Masterpasqua, & Joseph, 1995; Sandfort, 1998; Johnson, Wadsworth, Wellings, & Field, 1994). The high educational level among lesbian mothers may be associated with the pioneering position planned lesbian families have in society. The educational level of the heterosexual families involved in this study, however, is also relatively high. An over-representation of respondents with a high level of education in mail surveys has been reported before (e.g., Picavet, 2001; Siemiatycki, 1979). In our study an over-representation of respondents with a high level of education was found in both family types. Therefore, both groups are comparable on this aspect. An important limitation of the present study is that parenthood motives, reflection on parenthood motives and the strength of the desire to have children were examined retrospectively. According to Crespi (2001), most lesbian couples decide to have children many years before they actually take any action. Probably, the analytic decision-making process (e.g., seeking a donor), and the experiences of reproductive assistance (long waiting lists, and a conception process that takes a long time) may influence the scores of the lesbian mothers on the questionnaires.

In our study lesbian mothers were significantly older than heterosexual parents at the time they got their first child. There are several reasons why getting children at a later age is characteristic to lesbian parenthood. Lesbian couples who have decide to have children are confronted with seeking a sperm donor, and long waiting lists in fertility-clinics. Also, the actual conception process takes more time than getting pregnant by natural conception. Therefore, when significant difference between lesbian parents and heterosexual parents occurred, analysis of covariance were carried out using parental age at the time the first child was born, as the covariate.

It turns out that the hierarchy of parenthood motives of lesbian parents is quite similar to that of heterosexual parents. Lesbian parents (biological and social mothers) and heterosexual parents (mothers and fathers) score relatively high on motives such as happiness and parenthood, and relatively low on social control. Research on motives for parenthood among involuntarily childless couples (Van Balen & Trimbos-Kemper) and IVF-mothers (Colpin, de Munter, & Vandemeulebroecke, 1998) revealed similar findings. Just like among fertile heterosexual parents, happiness and parenthood were the most frequently mentioned categories of motives, while motives in the domain of continuity of family name were seldom mentioned (Weeda, 1989). Even though those studies examined a different group, the similarity in hierarch is not surprising. In Western societies motivations are part of the realm of expressions of personal development and involve notions of the unique parent-child relationship. Motives that express the interest of the group, social pressure, continuity or heredity are less important in Western societies nowadays (Van Balen & Inhorn, 2002).

Although the order of the motives was quite similar for lesbian and heterosexual parents, one motive (e.g., happiness) was more important, while most other motives were less important for the former than they were for the latter group. It is reasonable that for lesbian parents, who decided to have a child and had to go through years of procedures and waiting, happiness is more important as a motive because this motive might be more explicit and manifest for them than for fertile heterosexuals. Nonetheless, most other motives were less important for lesbian parents than for the control group of heterosexual parents. Motherhood identity as an aspect of achieving adulthood may be less important for lesbian than for heterosexual women (fertile and infertile), because lesbian women experience achieving adulthood primarily by the integration of the lesbian identity into a positive understanding of the self. Identity motives also refer to gender roles and these motives may be less important for lesbian women than they are for heterosexual men and women. Furthermore, in society, for heterosexual women the identity of being a mother is still evidence of their femininity (Morell, 1994; Ulrich & Weatherall, 2000). It was also found that for social mothers of the fist child who were biological mothers of subsequent children in the lesbian relationship, motives such as parenthood and continuity were more important compared to 'only social mothers.' It may be due to the experience of pregnancy and the bond with a biological child, the former group valued those parenthood motives more than the latter group.

The lesbian biological and social mothers spent more time thinking about the reasons for wanting to have children (reflection) compared to heterosexual parents, and the strength of their desire was also stronger for lesbian mothers. More reflection on parenthood motives may be a result of the socio-cultural context regarding homosexuality in general, and lesbian (and gay) parenthood in particular. De Graaf and Sandfort (2000) observed less favorable attitudes towards lesbian and gay men in their review of 73 research reports from the period 1990-2000 on the social position of lesbians and gay men in the Netherlands. Regarding parenthood, public opinion holds that a traditional family consisting of heterosexual partners – rather than of lesbian or gay partners – is the ideal environment to raise children in (Van Der Avort, Cuyvers, & De Hoog, 1996; Van De Meerendonk & Scheepers, in press). As a consequence of this socio-cultural context, for lesbian couples the transition to parenthood is a careful process of weighing pros and cons and taking implications into account (Touroni & Coyle, 2002). Furthermore, although the number of planned lesbian families has increased in recent years, parents in lesbian two-mother headed families are still pioneers in society. Perhaps, due to an awareness of this position, lesbian parents spent more time on the question why to have children. From anecdotal stories and small sample studies, it is known that the main concerns of lesbian women in their transition to parenthood are related to possible negative implications of raising a child in a non-traditional family in a heterosexist and homophobic society (Gartrell et al., 1996; Leiblum, Palmer, & Spector, 1995; Weeks, Heaphy, & Donovan, 2001). Lesbian women are concerned about their children's possible disadvantageous relationships outside the family caused by the prejudice encountered from their peers (Touroni & Coyle, 2002). However, research conducted among young adults who grew up in a lesbian-mother-family in the United Kingdom, demonstrated that as children they were not more likely than children having a heterosexual mother to be teased or bullied by peers (Golombok, 2000; Tasker & Golombok, 1997). In contrast, Vanfraussen et al. (2002) reported that children in lesbian families were teased more frequently than children in heterosexual families on family-related matters.

For lesbian biological and social mothers, but not for heterosexual parents an intense desire to have children correlated with a high reflection, and motives such as happiness and parenthood were significantly and positively correlated with reflection. Lesbian couples, like infertile heterosexual couples, have to go through a long and difficult process before they finally get pregnant, and the decision to have children is not taken easily (Gartell, et al., 1996; Touroni & Coyle, 2002). Several correlations were emerged between parenthood motives and strength of desire to have a child. The more important a motive was, the stronger the desire to have a child. In general, longing for happiness, parenthood-feelings and the optimization of well being correlated significantly with the desire to have a child. For lesbian biological mothers, however, only the motherhood motive (including items as parental feelings and the experience of pregnancy and birth) was significantly positively correlated with the strength of the desire to have a child. In this respect, it is interesting that Van Balen and Trimbos-Kemper (1995) in a group of involuntarily childless women also found that the expectation that parenthood would provide life-fulfillment was considerably more important.

For professionals who are assisting lesbian couples in the decision-making process on parenthood, these findings indicate the importance to reflect on and to discuss the desire for children and the meaning of a child with their lesbian clients.

Although there are differences in parenthood motives between lesbian and heterosexual parents, we can conclude that the hierarchy in parenthood motives in both groups is similar. Lesbian parents differed from heterosexual parents in that rethinking their motives for having a child and in the strength of their desire to have a child.

# IV

# Experience of parenthood, couple relationship, social support, and child rearing goals in planned lesbian families*

*The aim of this research was to examine whether planned lesbian mother families differ from heterosexual families on factors that are generally assumed to influence the parent-child relationship, such as experience of parenthood, child rearing goals, couple relationship, and social support. A total of 100 lesbian two-mother families were compared with 100 heterosexual families having naturally conceived children. A variety of measures were used to collect the data (questionnaires and a diary of activities). There are few differences between lesbian couples and heterosexual couples. Lesbian mothers appear less attuned to traditional childrearing goals and lesbian social mothers appear more to defend their position as mother.*

## 4.1  Introduction

The phenomenon of planned lesbian families (i.e., lesbians who have opted for motherhood within a lesbian relationship) is relatively new. Although the number of planned lesbian families in Western societies has been growing in recent years, little research has conducted on these families. The present article reports a study of planned lesbian families and compares them with heterosexual families on factors that are important, because they are assumed to influence the parent-child relationship, that is, as experience of parenthood, child rearing goals, couple relationship, and social support.

   In the past many women who were attracted to other women faced strong societal pressure to marry a man and have children. Same-sex feelings were repressed or expressed in a highly secretive way (Golombok, 2000; Slater, 1999). As a result of the gay liberation movement in the 1970s, increasing numbers of lesbians have abandoned secrecy. Lesbian women who had become a parent in a heterosexual relationship came out of the closet and openly identified themselves as lesbians (Blumenfeld & Raymond, 1988). After a divorce, they continued to raise their children, either alone or with same-sex partners. As a result of the increasing tolerance of homosexuality, an increasing number of women are becoming parents after coming out as a lesbian. Some of them are single mothers, while others

* This chapter is based on: Bos, H.M.W., Van Balen, F. & Van Den Boom, D.C. (2004). Experience of parenthood, couple relationship, social support, and child rearing goals in planned lesbian families. *Journal of Child Psychology and Psychiatry, 45*, 755-764.

are couples who planned their family together and share the parenting role (Golombok, 2000; Patterson, 1994; Patterson & Chan, 1999).

The majority of research has been conducted in lesbian families in which the mother initially raised the child in a previous heterosexual relationship. Lesbian families with children originating from a heterosexual relationship differ from planned lesbian families. In the former families the parental composition has changed, and parent and child experience divorce and coming-out of the mother. The present investigation is unique in that it focuses on a large group of planned lesbian families in order to eliminate the possible confounding effects of parental divorce, re-parenting, and coming out.

The few studies on planned lesbian families address the potential negative consequences for the developing child. The most common concern was that children's development with respect to sexual identity, mental health and social relationships would be impaired. Hence, researchers predominantly have posed questions concerning the developmental outcomes of children. Investigations in which planned lesbian families are compared with heterosexual families have, on the contrary, revealed no differences in child outcomes such as children's social competence (Flaks, Ficher, Masterpasqua & Joseph, 1995), behavioral adjustment (Brewaeys, Ponjaert, van Hall, & Golombok, 1997; Flaks, Ficher, Masterpasqua, & Joseph, 1995; Golombok, Tasker, & Murray, 1997), or gender role behavior (Brewaeys, Ponjaert, van Hall, & Golombok, 1997; Golombok et al., 2003). Only a few studies have focused on parenting behavior, finding indications that non-biological mothers in planned lesbian families have a higher quality of parent-child interaction (Brewaeys, Ponjaert, Van Hall, & Golombok, 1997; Golombok, Tasker, & Murray, 1997) and parenting awareness skills (Flaks, Ficher, Masterpasqua, & Joseph, 1995) than do fathers in heterosexual families. Furthermore, in most studies a pattern is observed in which lesbian partners in the two-mother families enjoy a higher level of synchronicity in parenting than partners within heterosexual families (Stacey & Biblarz, 2001). In heterosexual families, mothers score significantly higher than fathers on, for example, quality of parent-child interaction, but within the lesbian mother families there was no differences emerged between the two parents (Brewaeys, Ponjaert, Van Hall, & Golombok, 1997). No research has been conducted regarding the question whether planned lesbian families and heterosexual families differ on factors that are assumed to influence the parent-child relationship. The purpose of the present inquiry is to expand the knowledge – base on planned lesbian families regarding the factors experience of parenthood, couple relationship, social support, and child rearing goals.

The effects of social demographic characteristics on the parenting experience and family outcomes are widely investigated in heterosexual families. However, to out knowledge this was not examined before in lesbian families. In a more exploratory way, we therefore also examined the effect of social demographic characteristics on the parenting experience and family outcomes in lesbian families.

In the present study, planned lesbian families are compared with heterosexual families having natural conceived children. They were not compared with infertile heterosexual couples having a child conceived using new reproductive techniques, because the effect of the infertility experience in these couples is associated with a greater awareness of the importance of parenthood, and a stronger involvement in parenting (Van Balen & Trimbos-Kemper, 1995; Van Balen, 1996). Infertile heterosexual couples, particularly those who sought medical help to become pregnant, may also be very committed to parenthood (Golombok, Cook, Bish, & Murray, 1995; Van Balen, 1998).

In the Netherlands, where our study was carried out, there exists a relatively positive climate regarding homosexuality compared to other Western countries (Sandfort, 1998; Waaldijk, 1993; Widmer, Treas, & Newcomb, 1998). Contrary to this relatively positive climate, less favorable attitudes are still observed in the Netherlands regarding homosexuality and lesbian and gay parenthood (Van De Meerendonk & Scheepers, in press). Public opinion in the Netherlands still holds that a traditional family consisting of a heterosexual father and a mother is the ideal environment in which to raise children, and not to a lesbian or gay family (Van Der Avort, Cuyvers, & De Hoog, 1996; Van De Meerendonk & Scheepers, in press). Based on the idea that being a member of a minority group affects the lives of the members of that group (Goffman, 1963) various expectations are formulated regarding lesbian parenthood (Gillespie, 1999). As a consequence of a more negative public evaluation of same-sex families, lesbian mothers are thought to experience child rearing as extraordinarily difficult, resulting in parenting stress (Clarke, 2002). They also feel more pressured than heterosexual parents to justify the quality of parenthood (Morningstar, 1999; Rothuizen, 2001; Slater, 1999). Lesbian mothers must cope with a negative public opinion, which may have negative effects on the quality of the relationship (Weeks, Heaply, & Donovan, 2001). Although the number of planned lesbian families has increased in recent years, parents in lesbian two-headed families are still pioneers in society and it may be that the need of lesbian parents regarding child rearing support and child rearing guidance is higher. Because of the non-traditional family situation and minority situation, lesbian mothers probably also find other aspects important in the development of children. Such aspects as experiences of parenthood, quality of the relationship, social support or childrearing goals are important because they are supposed to influence the parent-child relationship (Cochran & Niegro, 1995; Goodnow & Collins, 1990; Meyers, 1999). However, the few empirical studies on planned lesbian families to date have, in general, not examined those aspects. Most of the studies on planned lesbian families employed are based on small samples. Samples were mainly recruited using one method, either through hospital fertility departments *or* through friendship networks. The present study avoids above pitfalls by examining a large sample of planned lesbian families – which were recruited with several methods – on factors that are supposed to influence the parent-child relationship, and compare them with heterosexual families.

## 4.2 Method

*Research Procedure*
Participation in the study for both the lesbian and the heterosexual families was based on the following criteria: (1) the children are raised in the family of origin from birth; (2) the age of the target child ranges from four to eight years; and (3) both parents are Dutch.

To ensure that the sample of lesbian families would not be selective and unrepresentative, lesbian mother families were recruited using several entries. The lesbian mother group was recruited first through the Medical Centre for Birth Control (MCBC), a centre providing artificial insemination services to clients regardless of sexual orientation or relationship status. The MCBC selected from its patients files, those two-mother headed families who had attended the clinic between 1992 and 1996 and who met our criteria for participation. Furthermore, lesbian families were selected from a mailing list of an interest group for gay and lesbian parents. This interest group is part of the most important and largest organization for gay and lesbians in the Netherlands (The N.V.I.H./COC). Most people on the mailing list are not a member of this organization. In addition, lesbian families were selected with the help of individuals with expertise in the area of gay and lesbian parenting (i.e., counselors working in the field of social work for gay and lesbian persons). Finally, an advertisement was placed in a lesbian magazine.

All selected lesbian families received an invitation to participate in the study, a letter of information, a reply-card and a stamped return envelope. Families willing to participate returned the reply card to the university.

The comparison group of heterosexual families was drawn from the population register of two cities. Heterosexual families were also contacted through schools and referrals from members of the lesbian family group. All selected heterosexual families received an invitation to participate similar to the one sent to the lesbian families and following to the same procedure. By means of the reply card we also obtained information on socio-demographic variables. It was, thus, possible to match the heterosexual families with the lesbian mother families on degree of urbanization, number of children, and age and gender of the target child.

*Response rate*
A letter of invitation was sent to 178 lesbian families. Of these, 43 were contacted through the MCBC, 60 through the interest group and 75 through experts in the area of gay and lesbian parenting. The total response rate for the lesbian family group was 99 (55.6%), for the medical centre 18 (41.9%), for the interest group 47 (78.3%) and for the experts 34 (45.3%). Only one family responded to the advertisement.

All in all, 1172 heterosexual families received a letter of invitation (the population registration offices: 600 families; schools: 510 families; referrals from participants of the lesbian family group: 62). Of these invitations, 251 (21.4%) were returned. For the population registration offices the response rate was 104 (17.3%), for schools 123 (24.1%) and for referrals from participants of the lesbian family group 24 (38.7%). From this pool of 251 heterosexual families, 100 were selected using our matching criteria (population registration offices: 42 families; schools: 49 families and referrals from participants of the lesbian family group: 9 families).

Differences were found between the overall response rates of the lesbian family group and of the heterosexual family group, that is, 55.6% and 21.4% respectively. The non-response rate among heterosexual families was expected to be higher than among lesbian families, based on the findings of previous research (Brewaeys, Ponjaert-Kristoffersen, Van Steirteghem, & Devroey, 1993; Jacob, Klock, & Maier, 1999; Wendland, Byrn, & Hill, 1996). Curiosity about the way lesbian parents function may have been an important reason for those couples to participate. The overall response rate among heterosexual families was normal using this research method (Brinkman, 2000; De Leeuw & De Heer, 2002).

*Instruments*

*Experiences of parenthood.* The NVOS – a Dutch questionnaire (Robbroeckx & Wels, 1989) for the measurement of family stress – was used to measure parental stress. Two dimensions were selected: parental burden (feeling burdened by the child) and parental competence (being able to handle the child). Examples of statements are 'Others (my partner) get too little attention because of my child' (parental burden) and 'I feel I'm slowly losing grip on my child' (parental competence). For both scales the items have response categories ranging from one (fully disagree) to five (fully agree). Wels and Robbroeckx (1991) judged the validity, internal consistency and stability of these subscales as good. In the present study Cronbach's alpha for parental burden was good ($\alpha = .81$) and Cronbach's alpha for parental competence was sufficient ($\alpha = .53$).

For this study, a new scale was developed to measure the extent to which parents believe that they must justify the quality of parenthood. This parental justification scale was based on theoretical considerations (Morningstar, 1999; Rothuizen, 2001; Slater, 1999), and the results of small qualitative studies on lesbian motherhood (Kaese & Gillespie, 1999; Seyda & Herrera, 1998, Warmerdam & Gort, 1998). The scale consists of four items (for example: 'In anticipation of negative reactions from others, I give my children more attention than other parents do'). Each item is scored on a 6-point scale, ranging from one (fully disagree) to six (fully agree). Cronbach's alpha on this scale was .68.

*Quality of the couple relationship.* Two dimensions covering the quality of the relationship were measured: satisfaction with the relationship and satisfaction with the partner as a co-parent. The Marital Satisfaction Scale (Gerris, et al., 1993) was used to provide a global assessment of couple relationship satisfaction. This scale is a 7-item questionnaire designed to measure spouses' overall satisfaction with their heterosexual marriage. It can, also be used for lesbian couples.

An example of a statement is 'If I had to make a choice again, I would choose the same partner'. Respondents were asked to indicate their agreement with the statements on a 6-point scale, ranging from one (completely disagree) to six (completely agree). Cronbach's alpha for this scale was .86. A subscale of the Parental Stress Index (Abidin, 1983; Groenendaal, Dekovic, & Noom, 1996) was used to measure the degree of satisfaction with the partner as a co-parent. This scale comprises 7 items (e.g., 'Since we have children, my partner has been less supporting than I expected'). Respondents were asked to indicate agreement with the statements on a 6-point scale, ranging from one (fully disagree) to six (fully agree). The reliability of this scale in the present study was .87.

*Social support.* The Vragenlijst Opvoedings Ondersteuning (VOO; Dekovic, Gerrits, Groenendaal, & Noom, 1996) – a Dutch questionnaire for the measurement of support with respect to child rearing practices – was used to measure how often respondents received informal (6 items) and formal social support (8 items). Informal social support comprises support from friends, neighbors and relatives. Formal social support is that provided by official authorities (e.g., schoolteachers) or the media. Items have response categories ranging from one (never) to six (everyday). The reliability of the two scales was .66 and .68, respectively.

To measure formal and informal social support, we also used two scales from the VOO to measured how satisfied respondents were with the support they received. The items had response categories ranging from one (dissatisfied) to five (satisfied). The reliability of these two scales was good: satisfaction with informal social support (6 items), $\alpha= .88$; satisfaction with formal social support (8 items), $\alpha= .83$.

*Child rearing goals.* The Child rearing Goals List developed by Vermulst, Gerris, and Siebenhaller (1987) was used to measure child rearing goals. This list consists of 45 items, each of which describes a quality or personality trait that parents want their children to develop. Although the List is a Q-sort method list, in the present study this list was included in the set of questionnaires. Respondents were asked to rate the importance of each item on a 4-point scale. The items have response categories ranging from one (completely unimportant) to four (very important). The subscale conformity (development of qualities that are valued as important in our society) consists of 23 items (e.g., 'self-control'). The reliability of this scale was good: $\alpha= .67$. The subscale autonomy (development of qualities that emphasize independence) consists of 12 items and the internal consistency was acceptable (Cronbach's' alpha= .63). The subscale development of a social personality turned out to be unreliable and was omitted from the analyses.

*Social demographic characteristics.* Data concerning social demographic characteristics (e.g., age and education) were also collected by means of questionnaires. Finally, how parents divided their time between work and family tasks was established by means of a structured diary record of activities. The diaries were divided into 15-minute time units and contained a checklist of activities, such as 'employment' for professional work and 'family tasks' for caring or help-ing children or preparing food. Respondents were asked to record the predomi-nant activity performed in each time unit and to record an event as soon as it occurred. Both parents completed the diary separately in an average week (Mon-day through Sunday) from 7:00 a.m. to 10:00 p.m. Although data collection using diaries has limitations (e.g., during the activities interruptions occur, activities overlap or an event is forgotten)(Ås, 1978; Kalfs, 1993), the diary format is valid and reliable (Kalfs, 1993). For each parent separately an Employment-Family Time Index was computed to measure the amount of time spent on work and on family tasks: hours per week of employment/(Hours per week of employment + household activities + childcare).

## Subjects

In lesbian families the biological mother of the target child was defined as the les-bian biological mother. The other mother was designated as the lesbian social mother. Hundred lesbian mother families and 100 heterosexual parent families participated in this study. Both groups were successfully matched on degree of urbanization, age, and gender of the target child. Most families in our study – both lesbian mother families and heterosexual parent families – lived in (sub)urban areas (91% versus 94%). Mean age of the target children did not differ signifi-cantly between the lesbian parent group and the heterosexual parent group ($M$=5.8 years, $SD$= 1.37 versus $M$=6.1 years, $SD$= 1.21); nor did the proportion of boys and girls (52 boys and 48 girls in the lesbian parent group, 51 boys and 49 girls in the heterosexual parent group) differ. Significant differences between the lesbian parent families and the heterosexual parent families were found for num-ber of children. The mean number of children in lesbian families ($M$= 1.87, $SD$= .51) is significantly lower than in heterosexual families ($M$= 2.03, $SD$= .48). However, the differences are small, $F (1, 198)$= 5.26, $p < .05$.

No significant differences were obtained on educational level of the parents. The majority of parents in both groups were highly educated (e.g., 75.5% of all respondents received education on a higher professional or academic level). There were, however, significant differences between the mean age of the lesbian biological mothers ($M$=40.8, $SD$= 3.22) and that of the heterosexual mothers ($M$=39.0, $SD$= 4.33), $F (1, 198)$= 11.54, $p < .001$, and between the mean age of the lesbian social mothers ($M$= 42.1, $SD$= 5.90) and that of the heterosexual fathers ($M$= 40.6, $SD$= 4.45), $F (1, 196)$= 3.98, $p < .05$. Furthermore, no significant differ-ences emerged between lesbian biological mothers and heterosexual mothers on the Employment-Family Time Index ($M$= .37, $SD$= .18 versus $M$= .33, $SD$= .16). In hours per week lesbian biological mothers spent on average 26.9 hours ($SD$= 13.08) on employment, and 44.9 hours ($SD$= 13.09) on family tasks. Heterosex-ual mothers spent on 24.0 hours per week ($SD$= 12.23) on employment and 46.8 hours per week ($SD$= 13.08) on family tasks. A significant difference was revealed on the Employment-Family Time Index between lesbian social mothers ($M$= .40, $SD$= .18) and heterosexual fathers ($M$= .60, $SD$= .13). The former spent more time on family tasks and less time on employment outside the home than the latter did, $F$ (1, 198)= 82.09, $p < .001$. Lesbian social mothers spent on average 29.41hours ($SD$= 13.96) and 42.2 hours ($SD$= 10.15) per week on employment and family tasks, respectively. The division of heterosexual fathers' hours per week on employment and family tasks was 43.1 ($SD$= 10.3) and 29.13 ($SD$= 9.69), respectively. Finally, the lesbian families and heterosexual families had relationships of similar duration: the lesbian couples had been together for an average of 14.9 years ($SD$= 3.87), the heterosexual couples for an average of 14.8 years ($SD$= 4.89).

*Data analysis*
Multivariate analyses of variance (MANOVA) were performed using all dependent variables to examine significant differences between the lesbian families and the heterosexual families. When Wilks' criterion was significant, a series of one-way ANOVAs were conducted in order to compare: (1) lesbian biological mothers with heterosexual mothers, and (2) lesbian social mothers with heterosexual fathers.

As mentioned at the beginning of this article, lesbian families and heterosexual families differ on parental age, the number of children in the family and the division of professional and childcare activities. These characteristics are more or linked to lesbian parenthood. Lesbian parents were expected to be significantly older than heterosexual parents. They start to consider having children at a later age than heterosexuals do. Conception requires much forethought, and donor insemination takes more time than getting pregnant by natural conception (Botchan et al., 2001). We also had reason to expect that in lesbian families the division of professional employment, practical childcare activities and household activities between both parents would be more equal than in heterosexual families (Brewaeys, Ponjaert, Van Hall, & Golombok, 1997). As a consequence of these differences between lesbian and heterosexual families, we decided that when one-way ANOVAs showed a significant difference between lesbian mothers and heterosexual parents, the initial group comparison was followed by an analyses of covariance using parental age, number of children, and the Employment-Family Time Index as covariates.

Paired t-tests were conducted to examine significant differences between biological mothers and social mothers in lesbian families, and mothers and fathers in heterosexual families.

To assess the relation between the variables examined and the social demographic characteristics of the lesbian parents (e.g., parental age, education and Employment-Family Time Index) correlation coefficients (Pearson's Product-Moment correlation r) were calculated between these variables, separately for lesbian biological mothers and lesbian social mothers.

## 4.3  Results

*Experience of parenthood, couple relationship, social support, and child rearing goals*

Multivariate analysis of variance was performed to investigated any significant differences between lesbian families and heterosexual families on all dependent variables. The results using Wilks' criterion showed a significant effect, $F(11, 321)= 3.56, p < .001$.

*Experience of parenthood*. No significant differences occurred between lesbian biological and heterosexual mothers on parental competence, parental burden and parental justification. Nor were significant differences obtained for parental competence and parental burden between lesbian social mothers on the one hand and heterosexual fathers on the other hand. There was, however, a significant difference between the rating of lesbian social mothers and heterosexual fathers on the parental justification scale. Lesbian social mothers reported significantly more often than fathers that they felt the need to justify the quality of their parenthood (see Table 4.1).

This effect remained after controlling for parental age, number of children and the Employment-Family Time Index, $F(1, 192)= 4.02, p < .05$.

Within the lesbian family group, there were no significant differences between biological mothers and social mothers on parental competence, parental burden and parental justification (experience of parenthood). Also within heterosexual families, both parents reported no significant differences on their experiences of parenthood.

Furthermore, it was analyzed for both lesbian biological and lesbian social mothers if social demographic characteristics of the lesbian parent showed a significant relation with parental competence, parental burden or parental justification. There appeared no significant correlations for lesbian social mothers. However, for lesbian biological mothers there appeared to be a significant correlation with the Employment-Family Time Index and parental burden ($r = -.20, p < .05$). Lesbian biological mothers feeling more often burdened by the child, were likely to spend more time on family tasks.

*Quality of couple relationship*. No significant difference emerged between lesbian biological mothers and heterosexual mothers on couple relationship satisfaction. There was a significant difference, however, between the way lesbian biological mothers and heterosexual mothers experienced the relationship with the partner as co-parent. Lesbian biological mothers were more satisfied with their partner as co-parent than heterosexual mothers were (see Table 4.1). After controlling for parental age, number of children and the Employment-Family Time Index, however, this effect disappeared. Although the differences between lesbian biological mothers and heterosexual mothers disappeared after controlling for covariates, none of the covariates had a significant contribution.

In comparison to heterosexual fathers, lesbian social mothers reported to be significantly more satisfied with the couple relationship. However, this difference

**Table 4.1  Parental experience of parenthood, couple relationship, social support, and child rearing goals**

| | Lesbian families | | | | Heterosexual families | | | | Lesbian biological mother versus heterosexual mothers | Lesbian social mother versus heterosexual fathers |
| | Biological mothers | | Social mothers | | Mothers | | Fathers | | | |
| | M | SD | M | SD | M | SD | M | SD | F-value | F-value |
|---|---|---|---|---|---|---|---|---|---|---|
| *Parental experience of parenthood* | | | | | | | | | | |
| Parental competence | 4.44 | .39 | 4.47 | .38 | 4.42 | .46 | 4.53 | .33 | .07 | 1.45 |
| Parental burden | 2.03 | .78 | 2.05 | .81 | 1.99 | .80 | 1.88 | .64 | .13 | 2.73 |
| Parental justification | 1.83 | .78 | 1.88 | .93 | 1.76 | .75 | 1.64 | .60 | .45 | 4.51* |
| *Quality of couple relationship* | | | | | | | | | | |
| Relationship satisfaction | 5.07 | .83 | 5.17 | .86 | 4.88 | .98 | 4.88 | 1.00 | 2.19 | 4.70* |
| Satisfaction partner as co-parent | 4.51 | .70 | 4.54 | .75 | 4.28 | .79 | 4.67 | .74 | 4.57* | .21 |
| *Social support* | | | | | | | | | | |
| Use of informal support | 2.18 | .54 | 2.14 | .59 | 2.28 | .70 | 1.97 | .65 | 1.28 | 3.63 |
| Use of formal support | 1.66 | .37 | 1.63 | .37 | 1.66 | .42 | 1.55 | .43 | .00 | 2.15 |
| Satisfaction informal support | 3.98 | .73 | 4.13 | .72 | 4.11 | .73 | 3.85 | .85 | 1.50 | 5.68** |
| Satisfaction formal support | 3.84 | .64 | 3.92 | .66 | 3.99 | .67 | 3.84 | .77 | 2.61 | .60 |
| *Child rearing goals* | | | | | | | | | | |
| Conformity | 2.38 | .18 | 2.42 | .20 | 2.49 | .22 | 2.50 | .19 | 14.08*** | 8.20** |
| Autonomy | 2.42 | .28 | 2.41 | .28 | 2.38 | .28 | 2.40 | .28 | 1.17 | .14 |

*p<.05;  **p<.01;  ***p<.001

was not significant after controlling for age of the parent, number of children and amount of time spent on work and family tasks. Although the significant effect disappeared after controlling for the covariates, none of the covariates had a significant contribution. With respect to satisfaction with the partner as a co-parent, no significant difference appeared between lesbian social mothers and heterosexual fathers (see Table 4.1).

Within the group of lesbian mother families, satisfaction with the couple relationship did not differ significantly between the biological and the social mother, nor was there a significant difference on satisfaction with their partner as a co-parent. Within the group of heterosexual families, no significant difference emerged between fathers and mothers on satisfaction with the relationship. Nevertheless mothers were significantly less satisfied with the partner as a co-parent than fathers were (paired samples t-test: df= 97, t= 4.84, $p < .001$).

Among lesbian biological mother no significant correlations emerged between socio-demographic characteristics on the one hand and couple relationship satisfaction and satisfaction with the partner as co-parent on the other hand. For lesbian social mothers, there was a negative correlation between education and satisfaction with the partner as a co-parent ($r= -.31, p < .01$). Lesbian social mothers having a higher level of education were less satisfied with their partner as a co-parent.

*Social support.* No significant differences were found between lesbian biological mothers and heterosexual mothers in their overall use of informal and formal social support in child rearing. Lesbian social mothers and heterosexual fathers also did not differ in overall use of social support, either formal or informal.

Furthermore, there were no significant differences between lesbian biological mothers and heterosexual mothers regarding satisfaction with available informal and formal social support. Lesbian social mothers, however, were significantly more satisfied than heterosexual fathers with the support received from friends, neighbors and relatives (informal social support)(see Table 4.1). After controlling for parental age, number of children and the Employment-Family Time Index, this relationship was not significant. Although the significant effect disappeared after controlling for the covariates, it appeared that none had a significant contribution in covariance analyses. Lesbian social mothers and heterosexual fathers did not differ significantly on satisfaction with formal social support (see Table 4.1).

Within the group of lesbian families the overall use of social support, both informal and formal, did not differ significantly between biological mothers and social mothers. This in contrast to differences obtained within the group of heterosexual families. Significantly more mothers than fathers reported using informal and formal social support with respect to child rearing (informal social support: paired samples t-test: df= 97, t= 3.30, $p < .001$; formal social support: paired samples t-test: df= 97, t= 2.11, $p < .05$).

Within the lesbian families, biological mothers and social mothers did not differ significantly with respect to satisfaction with the available formal and infor-

mal social support. Mothers in heterosexual families, however, were more satisfied with available informal social support than fathers were (paired samples t-
test: df= 97, t= 2.36, $p < .05$). Otherwise, parents in heterosexual families did not
significant differ on satisfaction with formal social support.

For lesbian biological mothers there appeared to be a significant correlation
between age of the parent and use of informal social support ($r= -.23, p < .05$).
Younger lesbian biological mothers, more often reported using support from
friends and neighbors. For lesbian social mothers, level of education was significantly correlated with the use of informal social support ($r= .25, p < .05$). Lesbian
social mothers with a higher level of education reported more often using social
support from, for example, friends.

*Child rearing goals.* Univariate analyses of variance with the group of lesbian
biological mothers and heterosexual mothers as the independent variable and
conformity as the dependent variable, showed that the former found it significantly less important for their child to develop qualities important in our society,
such as ambitions or self-control, than the latter group of mothers did (see Table
4.1). Analyse of covariance controlling for age of the parent, number of children
and the Employment-Family Time Index, showed that this relationship remained
significant, $F (1, 195)= 9.52, p < .01$. Lesbian social mothers also reported finding
these qualities significantly less important than heterosexual fathers did (see
Table 4.1). This difference remained significant after controlling for age of the
parent, number of children and Employment-Family Time Index, $F (1, 193)=
7.32, p < .01$.

There was no significant difference between lesbian biological mothers and
heterosexual mothers on the one hand, and between lesbian social mothers and
heterosexual fathers on the other hand on the scale that measuring the importance
of the development of qualities emphasizing children's independence (autonomy)(see Table 4.1).

Furthermore, within the group of lesbian families, no significant differences
were found between biological mothers and social mothers on child rearing
goals. Also within heterosexual families, there were no significant differences
between parents.

There appeared no significant correlations between social demographic variables and child rearing goals for lesbian biological mothers. However, significant
correlations were found for lesbian social mothers. Younger lesbian social mothers and lesbian social mothers having a higher level of education, were likely to
find conformity as less important ($r= .21, p <. 05$ and $r= -.21, p <. 05$) and autonomy more important ($r= .32, p <. 001$).

## 4.4 Discussion

The aim of this study was to investigate differences between planned lesbian families and heterosexual families having naturally conceived children on several
factors expected to influence the parent-child relationship. To do so, we investi-

gated 100 planned lesbian families and compared them with 100 heterosexual families on experiences of parenthood, quality of the couple relationship, social support and childrearing goals.

No confirmation was found for the expectation that, as a consequence of a negative evaluation of lesbian parenthood, lesbian mothers experience child rearing as more difficult. The findings revealed that lesbian mothers' experience of parental stress (parental burden and parental incompetence) were comparable to that of heterosexual parents. In addition, lesbian and heterosexual parents were comparable on using social support and on emphasizing independence in child development. Differences did emerged between lesbian mothers and heterosexual parents on relationship satisfaction and satisfaction with informal support. Apparently, the decision to pursue a less accepted lifestyle by society, wherein lesbians make the decision to become a mother within a lesbian relationship, results in a stable relationship (Giddens, 1992). This in contrast to findings on gay couples without children. According to Meyer (1989), the lack of support gay couples receive from their social network leads to instability in gay relationships. Significant differences found between lesbian and heterosexual parents on family outcomes disappeared when covariates were added, although, none of the covariates were significant. One should take into account that the control variables of parental age, the division of family tasks, employment and to a lesser extent number of children, are more or less naturally linked to lesbian parenthood.

One should also bear in mind that the educational level of the planned lesbian families is relatively high. On the other hand, other studies have also shown that lesbian women tend to be more highly educated (Steckel, 1987; McCandlish, 1987; Patterson, 1994; Flaks, Ficher, Masterpasqua, & Joseph, 1995; Sandfort, 1998; Johnson, Wadsworth, Wellings, & Field, 1994). Still, it seems that children from lesbian low-SES mother families are more likely than those from middle-class lesbian mother families to experience peer stigma about issues related to the lesbian identity of the mother (Tasker & Golombok, 1997).

Lesbian mothers and heterosexual parents differed remarkably on parental justification, and on the child rearing goal of conformity. That lesbian social mothers feel the need to justify the quality of parenthood, is probably due to the unique societal pressure these mothers feel to be visible as a mother (de Kanter, 1996; Muzio, 1999, Nekkebroeck & Brewaeys, 2002). Some prudence is required regarding this findings, because the instrument used to measure parents' believe to justify the quality of parenthood was a newly scale developed. Furthermore, lesbian parents score low on the child rearing goal of conformity. Previous inquiries also found that lesbians feel more comfortable discussing sexuality with their children, accepting their children's sexuality whatever it may be, and that teenage children of lesbians communicate their feelings more openly (Golombok, 2000; Tasker & Golombok, 1997). In addition, several authors suggest that children brought up by lesbian parents may benefit from their personal experience of diversity and may therefore feel less restricted (Patterson, 1992; Tasker & Golombok, 1997; Weeks, Heaphy, & Donovan, 2001).

Parents in lesbian families show a high level of synchronicity. There were no differences between lesbian biological and lesbian social mothers on the time they spent on childcare activities and activities, and on factors assumed to influence the parent-child relationship, such as parental stress or parental justification. In heterosexual families, however, mothers, spent more time than fathers on family tasks and mothers are less satisfied with their partner as a co-parent. This may enhance their need for social support from neighbors and friends. Perhaps, lesbian couples more easily operate on the basis of equality, because partners in lesbian couples create their relationships without reference to traditional roles and come into a relationships with a history of being socialized into the same gender role (Blumstein & Schwartz, 1983; Kurdek, 2001).

Finally, few correlations between socio demographic variables and parenting experience and family outcomes turned out to be significant for lesbian mothers. A pattern was found that highly-educated lesbian social mothers more often use informal social support. Furthermore, highly-educated lesbian social mothers showed less conformity in child rearing goals and also valued child independence more.

A limitation of the present study also found in other studies is the difference in response rate between the lesbian family group and the heterosexual family group, which was lower in the latter group (Breweays, Ponjaert, Van Hall, & Golombok, 1997; Jacob, Klock, & Maier, 1999; Wendland, Byrn, & Hill, 1996). Curiosity about the way lesbian parents function may have been an important reason for planned lesbian families to participate. In addition, all similarities and differences described in this study are based on self-reports by the parents. Although valid instruments were used, there is a possibility that an objective observations lead to different conclusions. However, we conclude that lesbian families and heterosexual families have much in common, expect that both family types differ on parental justification and child rearing goals.

# V

# Family characteristics, child rearing and child adjustment in planned lesbian families[*]

*The aim of this study was to compare planned lesbian families with heterosexual families on family characteristics, parental behavior, and child development. Hundred planned lesbian families were compared with 100 heterosexual families. Data was collected by means of questionnaires, observations of the parent-child relationship, and a diary of activities. The results show that lesbian social mothers differ from heterosexual father on family characteristics and parental behavior. It appears that characteristics that are more or less related to their attitudes as a social mother (for example: parental justification, and intensity of desire) were responsible for the observed differences between lesbian social mothers and heterosexual fathers on parental behavior, and not to the social mother herself. No differences were found between the psychological development of children in lesbian and those in heterosexual families.*

## 5.1  Introduction

In recent decades, the concept of what makes a "family" has changed dramatically. As a result of a number of social and demographic changes, Western societies are now made up of a multiplicity of family types in addition to the traditional nuclear two-parent family, such as one-parent families, patchwork or blended families, and lesbian families. These new family types offer the possibility to conduct "natural experiments" (Parke, 2004, page 388), and as such offer opportunities to explore and update our understanding of family functioning. The present article focuses on one of these new family types, namely planned lesbian families (i.e., lesbian two-mother families in which the child was born to the lesbian relationship). The necessity of rearing children in a home with both a male and a female parent was assessed by studying planned lesbian families in comparison with two-parent heterosexual families.

Opponents of lesbian parenthood, such as Cameron (1996), Wardle (1997), and Knight (1997), consider lesbian families to be both different and deviant from two-parent heterosexual families. In their view, children raised by active homosexual parents face certain unique risks of developing deviant gender and sexual identity. The social stigma and embarrassment of having a lesbian parent ostracize children and hinder their relationships with peers, resulting in emo-

---

[*] *This chapter is submitted for publication.*

tional problems. In the United States, these views continue to be cited in court decisions and policy hearings, despite the fact that empirical research comparing planned lesbian families with heterosexual families has revealed no differences in children's social competence (Flaks, Ficher, Masterpasqua, & Joseph, 1995), behavioral adjustment (Brewaeys, Ponjaert, van Hall, & Golombok, 1997; Flaks, Ficher, Masterpasqua, & Joseph, 1995; Golombok, Tasker, & Murray, 1997), or gender role behavior (Brewaeys, Ponjaert, van Hall, & Golombok, 1997; Golombok et al., 2003). However, these inquiries consisted of small samples, and in some studies single lesbian mothers and two-mother lesbian families were pooled. In contrast, the present study focuses on a large group of planned lesbian two mother families

In the few studies addressing parenting behavior in planned lesbian families, it was found that lesbian biological mothers did not differ from mothers in hetero-sexual families on the quality of parenting awareness skills (Flaks, Ficher, Masterpasqua, & Joseph, 1995), or the quality of parent-child interaction (Brewaeys, Ponjaert, van Hall, & Golombok, 1997; Flaks, Ficher, Masterpasqua, & Joseph, 1995; Golombok, Tasker & Murray, 1997). However, social mothers (non-bio-logical mother of the child) scored significantly higher on these aspects than het-erosexual fathers did, and they spent significantly more time performing family and childcare activities than did heterosexual fathers (Brewaeys, Ponjaert, van Hall, & Golombok, 1997; Golombok, Tasker, & Murray, 1997). Nevertheless, Golombok and colleagues (2003) showed that social mothers in lesbian mother families were less likely to display elevated levels of emotional involvement with their children than were fathers in fertile heterosexual couples. Although the chil-dren involved in that study were born to a lesbian relationship, the majority of the lesbian social mothers were stepmothers (Golombok et al., 2003). Stacey and Biblarz' (2001) review of studies on lesbian parenting showed that in heterosex-ual families, mothers scored significantly higher than fathers on synchronicity in parent-child interaction, while in lesbian mother families no differences were established. It should be borne in mind, however, that the aforementioned results were based on small samples using parental self-reports. The present study is unique because multiple sources of data collection were used, *viz.* questionnaires, diary methods, and observations.

Several authors (Brewaeys, Ponjaert, van Hall, & Golombok, 1997; Chan, Brooks, Raboy, & Patterson, 1998; Chan, Raboy, & Patterson, 1998; Flaks, Ficher, Masterpasqua, & Joseph, 1995) suggest that the comparative parenting strength that lesbian social mothers exhibit in comparison to heterosexual fathers, is related more to gender than to sexual orientation, that is, female gender is assumed to be the source of positive parenting skills. In general, mothers tend to be more involved in and skilled at childcare and parenting than fathers are (Furstenberg & Cherlin, 1991). In addition, research on lesbian parenting has revealed that lesbian biological mothers, lesbian social mothers, and heterosexual mothers have similar scores on measures related to child rearing (Brewaeys, Pon-jaert, van Hall, & Golombok, 1997; Chan, Brooks, Raboy, & Patterson, 1998;

Chan, Raboy, & Patterson, 1998; Flaks, Ficher, Masterpasqua, & Joseph, 1995). Stacey and Biblarz (2001), however, propose that the observed differences might be related to the nontraditional family composition of lesbian two-mother families that creates new kinds of family structures and processes that may have consequences for the parent-child relationship (Stacey & Biblarz, 2001; Dunne, 1999, 2000; Patterson, 1995; Patterson & Chan, 1999).

In two-women families, both mothers tend to spend the same amount of time on family tasks (i.e., childcare and household issues). This is not the case in heterosexual families. Hence, the finding that lesbian parents are more emotionally involved in their children might be because the division of family tasks and professional activities is more equal. The parent-child relationship could also be influenced by family characteristics unique to lesbian families. Lesbian parents are known to have a much stronger desire to have children because they have to cope with specific circumstances to reach that goal, such as a non-conventional way of getting pregnant, long waiting lists for donor insemination procedures in fertility- clinics, and more time to reflect on their choice as a result of a critical attitude from their environment (Bos, Van Balen, & Van Den Boom, 2003). It also takes more time to get pregnant through donor insemination than by having sex with one's partner, as is the case in a fertile heterosexual relationship. As a consequence, lesbian parents are usually older than heterosexual parents. Based on the idea that the desire to have children can profoundly influence parents' attitudes toward their child, and the parent-child relationship (Golombok, 1992; Colpin, 1994; Colpin, de Munter, & Vandemeulebroecke, 1998; Van Balen & Trimbos-Kemper, 1995), parenting differences between lesbian and heterosexual parents might also be caused by differences in the desire to have children and in parental age. Lesbian and heterosexual parents may also differ in the way they experience their parental role as a consequence of living in a society where less favorable attitudes toward lesbian and gay parenting predominate, resulting in defense mechanism regarding parenthood. Such mechanisms, in turn, influence parental behavior. Several authors suggest that lesbian parents are less focused on traditional parental behavioral goals than heterosexual parents are (Golombok, 2000; Patterson, 1992; Tasker & Golombok, 1997; Weeks, Heaphy, & Donovan, 2001). In sum, the fact that lesbian parents are more emotionally involved with their children than heterosexual parents are, might be mediated by such family characteristics as spending more time on family tasks, a stronger desire to have children, defense mechanisms toward parenthood, and deviations from traditional child rearing goals. Based on the literature, however, it is not clear which of these family characteristics is predominates.

In the literature, two dimensions have been consistently used to examine parental behavior (Baumrind, 1989; Maccoby & Martin, 1983), namely support and control. Support has been shown to be related to child adjustment. Control is subdivided into authoritative and restrictive control (Ten Haaf, Janssens, & Gerris, 1994). The former refers to encouraging the child's independence, and to reasoning and explaining, while the latter refers to setting limits and enforcing rules.

Research has shown that authoritative control has positive effects on the child's development, while restrictive control has negative effects (Grusec, Rudy, & Martini, 1997). In the present study, differences between planned lesbian parents and heterosexual parents were examined on the parenting behaviors support and control. In contrast to most other studies on planned lesbian families, multiple sources of data collection were used. Furthermore, most of the studies on planned lesbian families employed relatively small samples, and the samples were mainly recruited in one way, namely either through hospital fertility departments or through friendship networks. The present study avoided these pitfalls by examining a large sample of planned lesbian families recruited using several methods.

## 5.2 Method

*Participants*
The sample consisted of 100 planned lesbian families and 100 two-parent heterosexual families. Lesbian and heterosexual families were considered eligible to participate in the study if (1) the children had been raised in the family since birth, (2) one of the children (the target child) was between four and eight years of age, and (3) both parents were Dutch. To be able to make a meaningful comparison between lesbian and heterosexual families, both family types were matched on degree of urbanization, number of children, and age and gender of the target child. Families were not matched on parental age, because in general lesbian parents are older than heterosexual parents are. The data on the lesbian families were collected to be able to establish the socio-demographic context of the families. This information was then used to match the heterosexual families.

To obtain a representative sample of planned lesbian families, the group was recruited in several ways, namely through a medical centre for artificial insemination (response rate: 41.9%; N=18 couples), a mailing list of gay and lesbian parents (response rate: 78.3%; N=47 couples), and individuals with expertise in the area of gay and lesbian parenting (response rate: 45.3%; N=34 couples). Also, an advertisement was placed in a lesbian magazine. However, one family responded it.

The group of heterosexual families was drawn from the population register of two cities with a level of urbanization comparable to the cities in which the participating lesbian families lived, as well as through schools and referrals from the participating lesbian family group. The total response rate was 17.3% for the population register offices, 24.1% for the schools, and 38.7% for referrals. Using this procedure, we obtained a pool of 251 heterosexual families. Of these, 100 families were matched with the lesbian mother families (population registration offices: 42 families; professional contacts: 49 families; referrals: 9 families).

Lesbian families and heterosexual families were successfully matched on degree of urbanization and on age and gender of the target child. Both family types lived in a (sub)urban area (91% of the lesbian mother families and 94% of the heterosexual parent families), there was a similar proportion of boys and girls in each family type (52 boys and 48 girls in the lesbian mother group, 51 boys and 49 girls in the heterosexual parent group), and there were no significant differences between the two groups of families in mean age of the target child (lesbian families: $M=5.8$ years, $SD=1.37$; heterosexual families: $M=6.1$ years, $SD=1.21$). Mean number of children in the lesbian families ($M=1.87$, $SD=.51$), however, was significantly lower than in the heterosexual families ($M=2.03$, $SD=.48$), although the differences were small, $F(1, 198)=5.26$, $p < .05$.

No significant differences were established between lesbian parents and heterosexual parents on non-matched socio-demographic aspects, such as educational level (75.5% of all respondents had studied at a higher professional level) and duration of the relationship ($M=14.8$ years; $SD=4.39$). As expected, the lesbian biological mothers and social mothers were significantly older than the heterosexual mothers and fathers, $F(1, 198)=11.54$, $p < .001$, and $F(1, 196)=3.98$, $p < .05$, respectively.

*Procedure*
The families that agreed to participate in the study were contacted by phone to explain the three different methods of data collection (i.e., questionnaire, observations, and diaries), and to make an appointment for the home visit to observe parent-child interactions. Before the home visit, two questionnaires (one for each parent) were mailed. The parents were asked to fill out the questionnaires independently. Next, the family was visited at home at a time convenient to the parents. Parent-child observations were collected for both parents. Most home visits were made during the weekend. During the visit, parent and child were video-taped performing two instructional tasks. Parents were allowed to help the child whenever they felt the need to. During the visits, the parents were also taught how to fill in the diaries, which they were asked to return as soon as possible.

*Instruments and measures*
*Strength of the desire to have children.* The strength of parent's desire to have children (intensity of desire) was assessed on a six-point Likert-scale. The following question was posed: 'what were you willing to give up in order to have children?' (1=it didn't really matter to me-6= more than anything). The question referred to the first child.

*Child rearing goals.* A subscale of the Child rearing Goals List (Vermulst, Gerris, & Siebenhaller, 1987) was used to assess traditional child rearing goals (conformity). Although the list is a Q-sort method list, in the present study the list was included in the set of questionnaires. Respondents were asked to rate the importance of each item on a 4-point scale, ranging from 1 (completely unimportant) to 4 (very important). The subscale conformity (development of qualities that are valued in society) consists of 23 items (e.g., "self-control"). The reliability of this scale was good: $\alpha= .67$.

*Parental justification.* Parental justification – or the degree to which a parent experiences pressure to justify her/his quality of parenthood – was assessed by means of a newly developed scale, which was based on information obtained in small-scale qualitative studies of lesbian motherhood (Kaese & Gillespie, 1999; Seyda & Herrera, 1998, Rothuizen, 2001; Warmerdam & Gort, 1998). The scale consists of four items (e.g., "In anticipation of negative reactions from others, I give my children more attention than other parents do"), which are scored on a 6-point scale, ranging from 1 (fully disagree) to 6 (fully agree). Cronbach's alpha on this scale was .68.

*Division of work and family tasks.* This division of work and family tasks was assessed by means of a structured diary record of activities. Every 15 minutes, one activity was selected from a checklist of activities. The checklist was based on a classification system used in time budget surveys (CBS, 1999). Both parents completed the diary independently in an average week (Monday through Sunday) from 7:00 a.m. to 10:00 p.m. Based on the diary records, an Employment-Family Time Index was computed: hours per week of employment/(hours per week of employment + household activities + childcare). An index of zero indicates that a respondent spends no time on employment outside the home, but a lot of time on family tasks, while an index of 1 indicates that a parent spends no time on family tasks, but a lot of time on employment outside the home.

*Emotional involvement and parental concern.* Emotional involvement and parental concern were measured using the Child rearing Practices Report (CRPR; Block, 1965; Dekovic, 1991; van Balen, 1996). Van Balen (1996) combined original subscales from the CRPR to develop two scales, one measuring emotional involvement and the other measuring parental concern. Other researchers (Trickett & Susman, 1989; Kochanska, Kuczynski, & Radke-Yarrow, 1989, Dekovic, 1991) also combined subscales from the CRPR, as the original subscales consist of only a few items and the reliabilities were moderate or low. The parental emotional involvement scale (9 items; $\alpha =. 58$) consists of a combination of the subscales open expression of affection (e.g., "Express affection by kissing and hugging") and enjoyment of parental role (e.g., "Interesting to be with child for long periods"). The parental concern scale (10 items; $\alpha = .60$) consists of a combination of the original subscales parental worry about the child (e.g., "Worry about sad things that might happen"), protectiveness of child (e.g., "Keep child away from others with different values"), and over investment in child (e.g., "Tend to spoil child"). The items from both scales have response categories ranging from 1 (completely disagree) to 6 (completely agree).

*Power assertion and induction.* Power assertion and induction were measured using the Parenting Dimensions Inventory (PDI; Slater & Power, 1987; Gerrits, Dekovic, Groenendaal, & Noom, 1996; Gerrits, 2000). Power assertion refers to the degree to which parents use power assertive methods of discipline and control. Each parent was presented with six different situations describing potential misbehavior (e.g., "After arguing over toys, your child hits a playmate"), and was asked to indicate how likely it was (1 = very unlikely, 5 = very likely) that he/she would use physical punishment, yell at the child, ignore the child, withhold privileges, or send the child to his/her room. Induction measured the degree to which parents use inductive methods of discipline and control. The same situations were used as in the power assertion scale. For each situation, the parent was asked how likely it was (1 = very unlikely, 5 = very likely) that he/she would talk to the child, point out the consequences of the child's behavior, and point out earlier agreements. In the present study, the Cronbach alphas were .89 for power assertion and .87 for induction.

*Quality of parental interactive behavior.* Supportive presence, respect for the child's autonomy, and structure and limit-setting were assessed by rating the videotaped parent-child instruction sessions by means of the Erickson 7-point scales (Erickson, Sroufe & Egeland, 1985). Different raters, who had been trained by the first author, scored the observation situations. Scoring was blind, that is, without knowledge of the sexual orientation of the mother. Intercoder reliability, in terms of Cohen's kappa, was established for 38% of the interactions, and was computed for agreement within one scale point. The Cohen's kappa values were as follows: supportive presence .89; respect for the child's autonomy .92; structure and limit-setting .88.

*Child adjustment.* Behavioral problems were used as indices of child functioning and subsequently assessed by means of the Child Behavior Checklist (CBCL/4-18, Achenbach, 1991; Verhulst, van den Ende, & Koot, 1996). The CBCL includes 118 items. Each item is scored 0 if not true, 1 if somewhat true, and 2 if very true for their child. The sum of the scores on all items produces a total score reflecting an overall measure of the child's emotional/behavioral adjustment. The CBCL also produces a score for both internalizing and externalizing problem behavior. The alphas for the internalizing, externalizing, and total behavior scale were .82, .88, and .92, respectively. Scores on the following syndrome scales were also computed: withdraw, somatic complaints, anxious/depression, delinquent behavior, aggressive behavior, social problems, thought problems, and attention problems. In each family type, the sum of the scores of both parents on the CBCL scales (on the broad band and the narrow band scales) were pooled.

## 5.3 Results

A series of one-way ANOVAs was conducted to compare lesbian biological mothers with heterosexual mothers, and lesbian social mothers with heterosexual fathers, on a number of family characteristics (e.g., spending time on family tasks, desire to have children). The same analyses were conducted on parental behavior variables. Furthermore, two-way analyses of variance were conducted using family type and gender of the target child as independent variables, and the CBCL scales as dependent variables. Finally, it was investigated which family characteristic (e.g., spending time on family tasks, desire to have children) accounted for parental behavior differences between lesbian and heterosexual parents. Multiple regression analyses were computed to identify which of the family characteristics is determinative for these differences in parental behavior.

*Differences in family characteristics*

To compare lesbian biological mothers with heterosexual mothers on family characteristics, ANOVAs were conducted with family type as the independent variable and the Employment-Family Time Index, intensity of desire, parental justification, and conformity as dependent variables. Table 5.1 presents an overview of the means and standard deviations of all variables examined. The results show that lesbian biological mothers scored significantly higher than heterosexual mothers on the strength of the desire to have children, and that they found traditional child rearing goals less important.

ANOVAs with family type as the independent variable, and the Employment-Family Time Index, intensity of desire, parental justification, and conformity as dependent variables were also conducted to compare lesbian social mothers with heterosexual fathers. Significant differences emerged between lesbian social mothers and heterosexual fathers on most of the variables. As shown in Table 5.1, the results indicate that the lesbian social mothers' intensity of desire to have children was stronger than that of the heterosexual fathers. Lesbian social mothers felt significantly more often than heterosexual fathers that they had to justify the quality of their parenthood, and found traditional child rearing goals significantly less important. Finally, significant differences between lesbian social mothers and heterosexual fathers on the Employment-Family Time Index show that social mothers in lesbian families spend more time on family tasks than do fathers in heterosexual families.

*Differences in parental behavior*

To compare lesbian biological mothers with heterosexual mothers on parental behavior, ANOVAs were conducted with family type as the independent variable, and with emotional involvement, parental concern, power, induction, supportive presence, respect child's autonomy, and structure and limit-setting as dependent variables. Significant differences between lesbian biological mothers and heterosexual mothers were established only on structure and limit-setting (Table 5.1). These differences indicate that the lesbian biological mothers scored lower on structure and limit-setting than did the heterosexual mothers.

**Table 5.1 Means (SD) of family characteristics and parental behavior**

| | Lesbian biological mother | Heterosexual mother | F | Lesbian social mother | Heterosexual Father | F |
|---|---|---|---|---|---|---|
| *Family characteristics* | | | | | | |
| Employment-Family Time Index | .37 ( .18) | .33 ( .16) | 2.44 | .40 ( .18) | .60 ( .13) | 82.09*** |
| Intensity of desire | 4.52 ( .94) | 3.85 (1.18) | 19.87*** | 4.34 (1.08) | 3.57 (1.06) | 25.47*** |
| Parental justification | 1.83 ( .78) | 1.76 ( .75) | .45 | 1.88 ( .93) | 1.64 ( .60) | 4.51* |
| Conformity | 2.38 ( .18) | 2.49 ( .22) | 14.08*** | 2.42 ( .20) | 2.50 ( .19) | 8.20** |
| *Parental behavior* | | | | | | |
| Emotional involvement | 5.45 ( .35) | 5.34 ( .39) | 3.96 | 5.40 ( .39) | 5 26 ( .43) | 6.09** |
| Parental concern | 2.95 ( .57) | 2.88 ( .59) | .71 | 3.03 ( .67) | 2.80 ( .61) | 6.23** |
| Power | 1.77 ( .43) | 1.89 ( .48) | 3.56 | 1.71 ( .43) | 2.00 ( .53) | 18.02*** |
| Induction | 4.51 ( .47) | 4.52 ( .45) | .05 | 4.55 ( .51) | 4.41 ( .49) | 3.97* |
| Supportive presence | 5.44 (1.05) | 5.63 ( .87) | 1.99 | 5.34 (1.18) | 5.13 (1.17) | 1.57 |
| Respect for child's autonomy | 5.73 (1.05) | 5.66 ( .99) | .22 | 5.74 ( .91) | 5.03 (1.50) | 15.12** |
| Structure and limit setting | 5.65 (1.04) | 6.03 ( .61) | 9.95** | 5.34 (1.37) | 5.85 (1.11) | 8.15*** |

*$p<.05$;  **$p<.01$;  ***$p<.001$

ANOVAs using family type as the independent variable and the parental behavior variables mentioned above as dependent variables were conducted to compare lesbian social mothers with heterosexual fathers. As shown in Table 5.1, significant differences between lesbian social mothers and heterosexual fathers were found for parental concern and emotional involvement, with more involvement and concern reported by the lesbian social mothers. Furthermore, the social mothers reported more often the use of induction and showed more respect for the child's autonomy than heterosexual fathers did. However, with respect to power assertion, the opposite was found: lesbian social mothers reported less often using power assertion. This was also the case for structure and limit-setting: fathers scored significantly higher on this aspect than did the lesbian social mothers.

*Differences in child adjustment*

A series of 2 (family type: lesbian families vs. heterosexual families) x 2 (gender of the target child: boys vs. girls) ANOVAs wase used to assess differences in child adjustment between lesbian and heterosexual families. No significant main effects of family type were found on the total problem behavior scale, or on the internalizing and externalizing problem behavior scales (see Table 5.2). However, as shown in Table 5.2, significant main effects of gender of the target child were found on the total problem behavior scale and the externalizing problem behavior scale. Boys had a higher score on both the total behavior problem scale and the externalizing behavior problem scale. There was no significant family type x gender of the target child interaction on the total behavior problem scale, nor on the internalizing and externalizing behavior problem scales.

Additional analyses of syndrome scales (withdraw (I), somatic complaints (I), anxious/depression (I), social problems, thought problems, attention problems, delinquent behavior (E), aggressive behavior (E)) also yielded no significant main effect of family type (see Table 5.2). However, significant main effects of gender of the target child were found on somatic complaints, attention problems, and aggressive behavior. Girls had higher scores than boys on somatic complaints, while boys had higher scores on attention problems and aggressive behavior. No significant family type x gender of the target child interaction on the syndrome scales was found.

Table 5.2  Means (SD) of emotional behavior child adjustment in lesbian and heterosexual families, separately for boys and girls

| | Family Type | | | | | F value | | |
| | Lesbian Families | Heterosexual families | Total | | | Family type | Gender target child | Family type* gender target child |
|---|---|---|---|---|---|---|---|---|
| Withdraw | | | | | | .08 | .08 | 1.33 |
| Boys | 2.09 ( 1.60) | 2.37 ( 2.32) | 2.24 | ( 1.98) | | | | |
| Girls | 2.38 ( 2.06) | 2.20 ( 1.69) | 2.29 | ( 1.88) | | | | |
| Total | 2.24 ( 1.83) | 2.29 ( 2.02) | 2.26 | ( 1.93) | | | | |
| Somatic complaints | | | | | | .81 | 4.05 * | 1.80 |
| Boys | 1.25 ( 1.57) | 1.65 ( 2.13) | 1.45 | ( 1.87) | | | | |
| Girls | 1.84 ( 1.77) | 1.77 ( 1.53) | 1.80 | ( 1.65) | | | | |
| Total | 1.55 ( 1.69) | 1.71 ( 1.85) | 1.63 | ( 1.77) | | | | |
| Anxious/Depressed | | | | | | 3.24 | 1.13 | .30 |
| Boys | 2.14 ( 2.12) | 2.51 ( 2.51) | 2.32 | ( 2.77) | | | | |
| Girls | 2.29 ( 2.59) | 2.97 ( 3.29) | 2.63 | ( 2.98) | | | | |
| Total | 2.21 ( 2.35) | 2.74 ( 3.31) | 2.48 | ( 2.88) | | | | |
| Social problems | | | | | | .62 | 3.24 | .68 |
| Boys | 1.45 ( 1.64) | 1.72 ( 1.94) | 1.58 | ( 1.79) | | | | |
| Girls | 1.29 ( 1.40) | 1.29 ( 1.51) | 1.29 | ( 1.45) | | | | |
| Total | 1.37 ( 1.53) | 1.50 ( 1.74) | 1.44 | ( 1.64) | | | | |
| Thought problems | | | | | | 2.87 | .30 | .56 |
| Boys | .74 ( .99) | .99 ( 1.21) | .87 | ( 1.11) | | | | |
| Girls | .76 ( .94) | .86 ( .90) | .81 | ( .92) | | | | |
| Total | .75 ( .97) | .92 ( 1.06) | .84 | ( 1.02) | | | | |
| Attention problems | | | | | | 1.05 | 12.97*** | 1.83 |
| Boys | 3.03 ( 2.52) | 3.63 ( 3.12) | 3.33 | ( 2.84) | | | | |
| Girls | 2.48 ( 2.02) | 2.40 ( 2.07) | 2.44 | ( 2.44) | | | | |
| Total | 2.76 ( 2.31) | 3.01 ( 2.72) | 2.89 | ( 2.52) | | | | |

Table 5.2 Means (SD) of emotional behavior child adjustment in lesbian and heterosexual families, separately for boys and girls

| | Family Type | | | F value | | |
|---|---|---|---|---|---|---|
| | Lesbian Families | Heterosexual families | Total | Family type | Gender target child | Family type* gender target child |
| Delinquent behavior | | | | 1.95 | 3.06 | 1.87 |
| Boys | 1.33 ( 1.33) | 1.73 ( 1.70) | 1.53 ( 1.54) | | | |
| Girls | 1.27 ( 1.46) | 1.28 ( 1.28) | 1.27 ( 1.27) | | | |
| Total | 1.30 ( 1.39) | 1.50 ( 1.50) | 1.40 ( 1.46) | | | |
| Aggressive behavior | | | | .58 | 16.32*** | .06 |
| Boys | 8.29 ( 5.76) | 8.58 ( 6.83) | 8.43 ( 6.29) | | | |
| Girls | 5.85 ( 5.10) | 6.43 ( 4.63) | 6.14 ( 4.86) | | | |
| Total | 7.07 ( 5.57) | 7.50 ( 5.91) | 7.29 ( 5.74) | | | |
| Internalizing | | | | 1.67 | 1.85 | .33 |
| Boys | 5.45 ( 3.70) | 6.40 ( 6.45) | 5.93 ( 5.23) | | | |
| Girls | 6.44 ( 5.02) | 6.81 ( 4.84) | 6.62 ( 4.92) | | | |
| Total | 5.94 ( 4.40) | 6.61 ( 5.68) | 6.27 ( 5.08) | | | |
| Externalizing | | | | .78 | 13.95*** | .99 |
| Boys | 9.62 ( 6.70) | 10.22 ( 8.03) | 9.92 ( 7.37) | | | |
| Girls | 7.13 ( 6.25) | 7.70 ( 5.44) | 7.41 ( 5.85) | | | |
| Total | 8.37 ( 6.59) | 8.96 ( 6.97) | 8.66 ( 6.78) | | | |
| Total | | | | 1.85 | 4.96* | .46 |
| Boys | 20.38 (11.40) | 23.10 (17.88) | 21.74 (14.96) | | | |
| Girls | 18.30 (11.81) | 19.21 (11.04) | 18.76 (11.40) | | | |
| Total | 19.34 (11.62) | 21.16 (14.98) | 20.25 (13.41) | | | |

*$p<.05$; **$p<.01$; ***$p<.001$

*Predictors of parental behavior*

*Lesbian biological mothers and heterosexual mothers.* A multiple regression analysis was conducted to identify the factors that account for the observed difference in structure and limit-setting. Predictor variables were those socio-demographic and family characteristics on which lesbian biological mothers and heterosexual mothers differed, and the parents' sexual orientation.

As shown in Table 5.3, it was found that sexual orientation is still related to structure and limit-setting after controlling for parental age, number of children, desire to have children, and conformity, and that none of the socio-demographic and family characteristics is significantly related to structure and limit-setting.

**Table 5.3 Multiple regression analyses predicting differences in parental behavior between lesbian biological mothers and heterosexual mothers**

|  | Structure and limit setting |
| --- | --- |
| *Predictor* | |
| Parental age | -.09 |
| Number of children | .11 |
| Intensity of desire | .13 |
| Conformity | .02 |
| Sexual orientation | .22** |
| $R^2$ | .09** |

$*p<.05;$   $**p<.01;$   $***p<.001$

*Lesbian social mothers and heterosexual fathers.* Multiple regression analyses were conducted to identify the factors accounting for the observed differences in emotional involvement, parental concern, power, induction, respect for child's autonomy, and structure and limit-setting, with the aforementioned parental behaviors as dependent variables and using as predictor variables those socio-demographic variables and family characteristics on which lesbian social mothers and heterosexual fathers differed, and sexual orientation/ parental status. Table 5.4 presents the results of these analyses.

For emotional involvement, the significant effect of sexual orientation/ parental status disappeared after controlling for socio-demographic variables and family characteristics. The standard regression coefficients shown in Table 5.4 indicate that the strength of the desire made a significant contribution to the explained variance in emotional involvement. With respect to parental concern, the effects of sexual orientation/parental status disappeared after controlling for socio-demographic variables and family characteristics. Significant predictors of parental concern were the Employment-Family Time Index, parental justification, and traditional parental behavior goals. For induction, the effect of sexual

**Table 5.4 Multiple regression analyses predicting differences in parental behavior between lesbian social mothers and heterosexual fathers**

| | Emotional Involvement | Parental concern | Power | Induction | Structure and limit setting | Respect child's autonomy |
|---|---|---|---|---|---|---|
| *Predictor* | | | | | | |
| Parental age | .02 | .00 | -.06 | -.06 | -.17* | .15 |
| Number of children | -.11 | .07 | .07 | -.03 | .09 | .03 |
| Employment-Family Time Index | -.12 | -.16* | .13 | -.06 | .03 | -.06 |
| Intensity of desire | .27*** | .05 | -.04 | -.04 | -.13 | -.03 |
| Parental justification | -.08 | .19** | .21** | -.04 | .01 | -.02 |
| Conformity | -.04 | .31*** | .15* | .14 | .07 | -.22*** |
| Sexual orientation/ parental status | -.02 | -.12 | .18* | -.17 | .06 | -.19* |
| R² | .11** | .20*** | .17*** | .05 | .16*** | .16*** |

*p<.05;  **p<.01;  ***p<.001

orientation/parental status disappeared after controlling for the various socio-demographic and other family characteristics. However, none of the variables appeared to make a significant contribution. The significant association found between sexual orientation/parental status and structure and limit-setting also disappeared after controlling for socio-demographic variables and family characteristics. Structure and limit-setting was significantly related to parental age. Findings on power assertion, however, show that sexual orientation/parental status is still related to power assertion after controlling for socio-demographic variables and family characteristics, although power assertion is significantly related to parental justification and traditional child rearing goals. Finally, as regards respecting the child's autonomy, sexual orientation/parental status is still related to this aspect after controlling for socio-demographic variables and family characteristics. Respecting the child's autonomy is also significantly related to parental age and conformity as a child rearing goal.

## 5.4 Discussion

Lesbian biological mothers and heterosexual mothers differ on only one of the aspects of parental behavior investigated, namely structure and limit-setting. Lesbian social mothers and heterosexual fathers differ on almost all aspects of parental behavior examined. However, the differences seemed to be mediated by family characteristics (e.g., parental justification, spending time on family tasks, stronger desire to have children). No differences in child adjustment were found between children in lesbian and those in heterosexual families.

The reason that there is virtually no difference between lesbian biological mothers and heterosexual mothers as regards parental behaviors may be that female gender is the source of positive parenting skills (Bussey & Bandura, 1999; Furstenberg & Cherlin, 1991; Simons et al., 1996; Youniss & Smollar, 1985). This might be related to the importance women attach to interpersonal responsibilities (Chodorow, 1978; Gilligan, 1982).

For lesbian social and heterosexual fathers, sexual orientation/parental status seems to have an effect on two of the parental behaviors investigated, namely power assertion and respecting the child's autonomy. However, it is unclear whether these differences can be attributed to sexual orientation, gender, or the difference in genetic tie. Lesbian social mothers and heterosexual fathers differ on all three aspects. Differences between lesbian social mothers and heterosexual fathers on the other parental behaviors are mediated by a high score on family tasks involvement, desire to have children, and defense mechanisms toward parenthood (parental justification), and a lower score on traditional child rearing goals. However, it seems that parental justification played the most important role. An explanation might be that lesbian social mothers differ from heterosexual fathers on these mediated variables because of the unique position of the former: Lesbian social mothers are not biologically related to the child, and for them becoming a parent had been a more complex matter than it had been for the heterosexual fathers. It also may have to do with differences in gender. Furthermore, the position of lesbian social mothers does not fit into the larger societal definition of what constitutes a family and, therefore, lesbian social mothers might feel a unique societal pressure to be a good mother (De Kanter, 1996; Muzio, 1999; Nekkebroeck & Brewaeys, 2002).

These findings seem to contradict those recently reported by Golombok and colleagues (2003), who found that lesbian social mothers were less likely to show enhanced levels of emotional involvement in their children than fathers in heterosexual families. This might be related to the fact that in their study, a substantial number of the lesbian social mothers were stepmothers. This is in contrast with the present study, in which all the social mothers had raised the child since birth and had been actively involved in the decision to have a child within the relationship with the biological mother of the child.

With respect to child adjustment, our findings support the results of studies based on small sample sizes. Children in lesbian mother families did not differ from children raised in heterosexual families on emotional and behavioral adjustment. Research by Flaks and colleagues (1995) substantiates what we found in our study, namely that children in heterosexual families do not differ from children in lesbian families in terms of problem behavior. Our result is in line with the view of Roberts and Strayer (1987), who assume that higher levels of warmth and parental involvement do not result in increasing levels of well being of a child once a certain threshold has been passed. Our findings are also in line with the results among other parents who also have go through great lengths before they could fulfill their wish to create a family, such as IVF, AID, and adoptive parents (Golomok et al., 1995; Van Balen, 1998). In addition, how children grow up and develop is influenced by many other factors, such as genetics and the influence of friends and peer groups (Maccoby, 2000). Furthermore, it was found that boys appear to have more problem behaviors than girls. However, this was the case in both lesbian and heterosexual families. Our findings contradict what is maintained by opponents of lesbian parenthood (Cameron, 1996a, 1996b; Wardle, 1997, Knight, 1997).

It should be mentioned that in the present study there was a difference in response rate between the lesbian and the heterosexual families. The non-response rate among the latter group was expected to be higher than among the former, based on findings of previous research (Brewaeys, Ponjaert-Kristoffersen, Van Steirteghem, & Devroey, 1993; Jacob, Klock, & Maier, 1999; Wendland, Byrn, & Hill, 1996). Curiosity about the way lesbian parents function might have been an important reason for those couples to participate. However, the response rate in our study among heterosexual families was comparable with that in other Dutch studies on family issues (Brinkman, 2000; De Leeuw & De Heer, 2002).

Furthermore, the educational level of the planned lesbian families involved in the present study is high. However, several studies have shown that lesbian women tend to be more highly educated than average (Steckel, 1987; McCandlish, 1987; Patterson, 1994; Flaks, Ficher, Masterpasqua, & Joseph, 1995; Sandfort, 1998; Johnson, Wadsworth, Wellings, & Field, 1994). The educational level of the heterosexual families involved in this study is also relatively high; therefore the lesbian and the heterosexual families were comparable on this aspect.

In conclusion, it appears that the family characteristics that are more or less representative of lesbian social mothers are responsible for the observed differences in parental behaviors between lesbian social mothers and heterosexual fathers. Where differences in parental behavior between lesbian social mothers and heterosexual fathers still exist after controlling for family characteristics, it is unclear whether these differences can be attributed to sexual orientation, gender, or the difference in genetic tie. Therefore, future studies should compare planned lesbian families, heterosexual families, and gay father families to further resolve this issue.

# VI

# Minority stress, experiences of parenthood, and child adjustment*

*The aim of this study was to explore the relationship of minority stress with experiences of parenthood and child adjustment in lesbian mother families. Hundred planned lesbian families involved in this study. Data were collected by means of written questionnaire. The lesbian mothers generally described low levels of rejection, they perceived little stigmatization, and they also manifested low levels of internalized homophobia. However, minority stress (especially experiences of rejection) was significantly related to experiences of parenthood and children's behavior problems.*

## 6.1 Introduction

Research on two-mother families has mainly focused on consequences for the child of living in a family with two mothers, compared to families consisting of a mother and a father. In the literature two-mother families in which the child was born to the lesbian relationship are characterized as 'planned lesbian mother families' (Flaks, Ficher, Masterpasqua, & Joseph, 1995, p 105). In this relatively new family type, the two lesbian mothers (the biological mother and the social mother) planned their children together. This in contrast to lesbian families were children were born in a previous heterosexual relationship. Existing research considers planned lesbian families primarily as a homogenous group. There are, however, important differences within planned lesbian families. Heterogeneity might, for instance, result from experiences lesbian mothers encounter with negative attitudes regarding their non-traditional family situation, and one's own attitude toward being lesbian. Such experiences can be assessed as stressors and have been defined as minority stress (Brooks, 1981; DiPlacido, 1998; Meyer, 1995, 2003a, 2003b). The aim of the present inquiry is to examine the relationship of minority stress with experiences of parenthood and child adjustment in planned lesbian families.

Studies that considered planned lesbian families as a homogenous group, have revealed no differences in child outcomes such as social competence, behavioral adjustment, and gender identity between children in lesbian and heterosexual families (e.g., Golombok et al., 2003; Brewaeys, Ponjaert, Van Hall, & Golom-

* This chapter is based on: Bos, H.M.W., Van Balen, F. & Van Den Boom, D.C. (in press). Minority stress, experiences of parenthood, and child adjustment. *Journal of Reproductive and Infant Psychology*.

bok, 1997). The few studies that focused on parenting behavior, found indications that the non-biological mothers (e.g., social mothers) in planned lesbian families show a higher quality of parent-child interaction (Brewaeys, Ponjaert, Van Hall & Golombok, 1997; Golombok, Tasker, & Murray, 1997) and parenting awareness skills (Flaks, Ficher, Masterpasqua, & Joseph, 1995) than do fathers in heterosexual families. Furthermore, within the lesbian families there was no difference between the biological mother and the social mother in quality of parent-child interaction (Brewaeys, Ponjaert, Van Hall, & Golombok, 1997).

Little is yet known, for example, about sources of differences within lesbian families. Patterson (1995b) found that when lesbian mothers shared the labor involved in childcare more evenly, they reported a higher level of well being of their children. Another study reported that lesbian mothers who described their own psychological adjustment and self-esteem in positive terms were also more likely to report that their children were developing well (Patterson, 2001). However, research on diversity in families with lesbian parents and potential effects of such diversity on children is scarce. Little is known about the influence of minority stress on experiences of lesbian mothers.

Contextual sources of stress are major determinants of parenting, and these stressors can also both directly and indirectly influence children's adjustment. Research on diversity within heterosexual families has typically involved assessment of the adverse impact of difficult life circumstances such as low SES (e.g. Werner & Smith, 1982), single parenting (Weinraub, & Wolf, 1983) and major negative life changes (Crnic, Greenberg, Ragozin, Robinson, & Basham, 1983). In sum, these studies found that parents experience high levels of stress are less satisfied with parenting, and high level of is associated with low levels of child adjustment. Research further suggests that daily hassles, as appraised by the individual parent, are important predictors of child outcomes (Österber & Hagekull, 2000). In everyday life, mothers in lesbian families experience stigmatization and negative events related to their sexual orientation or non-traditional lifestyle. This in contrast to parents in heterosexual families. These experiences can be seen as important daily stressors for lesbian mothers, and because of their potential negative effects they should be studied with high priority.

Minority stress can be distinguished into several dimensions, such as actual negative experiences (i.e., rejection), expectations of rejection and discrimination (i.e., perceived stigma), and internalized homophobia. Research has shown that lesbians and gay men are frequently exposed to prejudice events, including antigay/lesbian violence, discrimination, subtle forms of exclusion, and confrontation with negative attitudes regarding their non-traditional lifestyle (Mays & Cochran, 2001; De Graaf & Sandfort, 2000; Sandfort, Bos, & Vet, in press). In addition to negative experiences that gay men and lesbian women experience in general, lesbian mothers have to deal with less favorable attitudes towards lesbian motherhood. In the Netherlands, where the present study is conducted, public opinion holds that a traditional family is the ideal environment to raise children – in contrast to a lesbian or gay family (Van Der Avort, Cuyvers, & De Hoog,

1996) – and dominant public opinion is not in favor of equal rights for lesbians when it comes to adopting children (Van De Meerendonk & Scheepers, in press). King and Black (1999) show that college students in the U.S. expect that children of lesbian mothers display more behavior problems than other children. Lesbian mothers learn to anticipate on such negative attitudes by perceiving that they are not really accepted by other people in society and they, therefore, avoid seeking contact. As a consequence, lesbians and gay men might think that society in general and specifically heterosexual people disrespect them because of their non-traditional lifestyle. To characterize these expectations of negative treatment, the term perceived stigma has been introduced (Meyer, 1995; Ross & Rosser, 1996; Herek & Glunt, 1995).

Long before lesbian women begin to realize their same-sex feelings, some have internalized societal antihomosexual attitudes (Shildo, 1994). This is called internalized homophobia, and represents a form of internalized stress. Even in the absence of negative events, and even if one's minority status is successfully concealed, lesbians may under stress due to negative self-evaluations (Meyer, 2003a, 2003b). Internalized homophobia, can been seen as the homosexual opposite of self-esteem (Sandfort, 2000). Internalized homophobia consists of negative attitudes towards one's own homosexuality, as well as negative attitudes toward other homosexual persons (Shidlo, 1994; Szymanski, Chung, & Balsam, 2001).

The influence of minority stress on lesbian women and gay men has been examined in various studies. Several studies in the U.S and also in the Netherlands, demonstrated a relationship between homo-negative experiences and on adverse psychological health status (Sandfort & Bos, 2000; Sandfort, Bos, & Vet, in press; Waldo, 1999). In the workplace, for example, lesbian women who reported more rejection attributed to their homosexuality were less satisfied with their job (Sandfort, Bos, & Vet, in press). The internalization of negative attitudes towards lesbian women and gay men have been found to be related to an array of mental health problems, including depression, alcoholism, and sexual dysfunction (see for a review: Meyer, 2003a). Lesbian families, however, have not previously been examined from the perspective of minority stress.

In the present study we examined the extent to which lesbian mothers experience minority stress. We also investigated various hypotheses regarding the associations between minority stress and experiences of parenthood and child adjustment. Our hypotheses were based on the idea that being a member of a differently valued minority group negatively affects the lives of the members of that group (Goffman, 1963). We hypothesized that lesbian mothers who experience more rejection, and experience higher levels of perceived stigma and internalized homophobia would experience parenthood as more stressful. These mothers also feel a stronger need to justify the quality of parenthood. It was further hypothesized that children with lesbian mothers who experience more minority stress would be less well adjusted.

## 6.2 Method

*Participants*
*Eligibility and Recruitment of Families.* Lesbian families were considered eligible to participate in this study if the children were raised in two-mother lesbian families from birth. One of the children in the families had to be between four to eight years old, and with respect to this child (i.e., target child) parental experience of parenthood and child adjustment is examined in the present study. In cases that there were more children between four to eight years old, one of them was randomly pointed out as the target child by the first author.

Recruitment proceeded using four different strategies. We used the patient files of the Medical Center for Birth Control (MCBC), a center providing artificial insemination services to clients regardless of sexual orientation or the existence of an intimate relationship. In addition, families were recruited with the help of the largest interest group for gay and lesbian parents. Furthermore, lesbian families were selected with the help of individuals with expertise in the area of gay and lesbian parenting. We also placed an advertisement in a lesbian magazine.

A letter of invitation was sent to 178 lesbian families. These families were selected because they met our criteria for participation. Of the 178 lesbian families contacted, 43 came from the MCBC, 60 from the interest group and 75 from experts in the area of gay and lesbian parenting. The total response rate was 99 (55.6%), for the medical centre 18 (41.9%), for the interest group 47 (78.3%) and for the experts 34 (45.3%). One family responded to the advertisement.

*Participating Families.* Hundred two-mother families participated in the study. The biological mother of the target child (e.g., the child that the mother reflected on when she answering the questionnaire) was designated as the biological mother, while the other mother was designated as the social mother.

Biological mothers were older than social mothers, although the difference was not significant (Biological mothers: mean age 40.80, $SD=3.22$; Social mothers: mean age 42.10, $SD=5.90$). Most biological mothers and social mothers were well educated (e.g., 75.5% of all mothers received a higher professional or academic degree), and both mothers did not differ significantly on educational level. The age at which biological and social mothers openly identified themselves as a lesbian (e.g., coming-out) was 21.43 ($SD=4,86$) and 21.08 ($SD=5.30$), respectively. Biological and social mothers did not differ significantly on this aspect. The lesbian couples lived together for an average of 14.9 years ($SD=3.87$). Most families (91%) lived in an urban environment. Mean number of children in the families was 2.0 ($SD=.48$). In each family, the target child was between 4 and 8 years of age ($M=5.8$; $SD=1.37$). There were 48 girls and 52 boys, who participated.

*Materials*
Participants completed a written questionnaire that contained items on minority stress, experience of parenthood, and child adjustment. Both parents completed the questionnaire independently. Almost all variables were measured by scales,

most of which had been used in other studies or were derived from scales success-fully used by others. Standardized instruments with good psychometric proper-ties were included.

*Minority stress.* The occurrence of rejection was assessed with a seven-item scale, based on the 'Leidse Mobbing Schaal' (LEMS; Hubert, 1996) and the Ley-mann Inventory of Psychological Terrorization (LIPT; Leymann, 1990). The LEMS and LIPT are two large scales that measure experience of rejection at work. Because of the length of these scales, the number of items was reduced and those items were selected that specifically referred to ridiculing, marginalizing, or exclusion. Furthermore, we reformulated the selected items in such a way that they applied to experiences from parents experiencing rejection in the social environment. Examples of items are: 'People called you names in relation to being a lesbian mother' and 'People asked annoying questions about your non-traditional family situation.' Respondents were asked to indicate on a 3-point scale (1= never and 3= regularly) how frequent the various forms of rejection had occurred in the previous year. Cronbach's alpha for rejection was good ($\alpha$ = .72).

The 'Samen of Apart' questionnaire (SAP; Sandfort, 1997) a Dutch question-naire on the way lesbian and gay men think about being gay or lesbian was used to measure perceived stigma and internalized homophobia. This assessment was develop by Sandfort (1997) and derived from existing instruments (Herek & Glunt, 1995; Herek, Cogan, Gillis, & Glunt, 1997; Ross & Rosser, 1996). In sev-eral studies (Sandfort, 1997; Bos & Sandfort, 1999) the validity and internal con-sistency of this questionnaire was good. With respect to perceived stigma, expected social stigma and assumptions about heterosexual's attitudes towards homosexuality (i.e., assumed heterosexuals' attitudes) were measured. Examples of statements are 'Repression of homosexuality still occurs, even in the Nether-lands' (expected social stigma) and 'Most straight people disapprove off homo-sexuality' (assumed heterosexuals' attitudes). In the present study Cronbach's alpha for expected social stigma was good ($\alpha$ = .77; four items) and Cronbach's alpha for assumed heterosexuals' attitudes was sufficient ($\alpha$ =. 69; six items).

The Internalized homophobia (IHP) scale includes negative attitudes and feel-ings against one's own homosexuality as well as negative attitudes and feelings against other lesbians and gay men (Nungesser, 1983; Shildo, 1994; Szymanski, Chung, & Balsam, 2001). In the present study both forms of IHP were assessed. The scale that measured negative attitudes toward one's own homosexuality (IHP directed to self) consisted of five items. Respondents had to indicate on a five-point scale agreement with the statement, ranging from one (fully disagree) to five (fully agree). Examples of items are 'Because I am a lesbian, I cannot really be myself', and 'I rather would not be lesbian'. The alpha for this scale was .67. The scale that measured negative attitudes towards other lesbians and gay men (IHP directed to others) consists of six items. An example is 'When I see certain lesbians on television, I don't want to belong to them' (1=fully disagree- 5= fully agree). The reliability of this scale was .73.

*Experiences of parenthood.* The Nijmegen questionnaire on child rearing circumstances (Nijmeegse vragenlijst voor de opvoedingssituatie NVOS; Rob-broeckx & Wels, 1989) for the measurement of family stress was used to measure parental stress. Two dimensions were selected: parental burden (feeling burdened by the child) and parental competence (being able to handle the child). Examples of statements are 'Others (my partner) get too little attention because of my child' (parental burden) and 'I feel I'm slowly losing grip on my child' (parental competence). The items of both scales have response categories ranging from one (fully disagree) to five (fully agree). Wels and Robbroeckx (1991) showed that the validity, internal consistency and stability of the subscales are good. Cronbach's alpha for parental burden was good ($\alpha = .82$) and for parental competence sufficient ($\alpha = .50$).

Small qualitative studies about lesbian motherhood (Kaese & Gillespie, 1999; Morningstar, 1999; Rothuizen, 2001; Seyda & Herrera, 1998, Slater, 1999; Warmerdam & Gort, 1998) showed that lesbian mothers frequently reported that they feel pressured to justify the quality of parenthood toward other people in the social environment. Due to the absence of a scale to measure feelings of parental justification, we developed one to assess these feelings. The scale consists of four items (for example: 'In anticipation of negative reactions from others, I give my children more attention than other parents do'). Each item is scored on a 6-point scale, ranging from one (fully disagree) to six (fully agree). Cronbach's alpha for this scale was $.70\alpha$.

*Child adjustment.* Children's emotional/ behavioral problems were used as indices of children's functioning and were assessed by using a Dutch translation of the Child Behavior Checklist for age 4-18 years (CBCL/4-18, Achenbach, 1991; Verhulst, van den Ende, & Koot, 1996). The CBCL is a widely used and well-validated instrument for the assessment of children's emotional/ behavioral problems on the basis of reports of parents. The CBCL includes 118 behavior problem items, and each is scored '0' if not true, '1' if somewhat true, and '2' if very true of the child. Emotional/ behavioral problems consists of two broadband scales (viz. internalizing and externalizing), and a total behavior-problem scale. The CBCL also includes items on social competence, however, Verhulst and his colleagues (1996) showed that this scale has limited reliability for children younger than 6 years old. Therefore, the social competence scale was not included in the present study. The alphas for the internalizing, externalizing and total behavior problem scale were .78, .87, and .89 respectively.

## 6.3 Results

*Descriptive Statistics*

Table 6.1 presents the means and standard deviations of biological and social mothers' scores on the dimensions of minority stress, experiences of parenthood, and child adjustment. To examine differences between biological and social mothers paired t-tests were carried out. Table 6.1 also presents the results of these paired t-test.

*Minority stress.* Biological mothers and social mothers did not differ significantly on actual negative experiences. Nor were significant differences obtained between biological mothers and social mothers on the expected social stigma and assumed heterosexuals' attitudes. With respect to negative attitudes toward one's own homosexuality and negative attitudes against other lesbians and gay men, biological and social mothers also did not differ significantly.

The most frequently reported form of rejection was other people asked annoying questions that were related to the lifestyle of the lesbian mothers (see Figure 6.1). Sixty-eight percent of the biological mothers and 72% of the social mothers reported this. Another frequently reported experience was other people gossiping about the non-traditional family lifestyle of the respondents (27.3% of the biological mothers and 32.7% of the social mothers). Somewhat less frequently reported experiences were disapproving comments related to the family situation (13% of the biological mothers and 12.1% of the social mothers) and exclusion by other people (12% of the biological mothers and 9.1% of the social mothers). Smaller proportions of respondents reported other forms of experiences with rejection. Biological and social mothers did not differ significantly on the different forms of rejection.

**Table 6.1 Minority Stress, and Emotional/ behavioral Adjustment of Children (mean and standard deviations), for Biological Mothers and Social Mothers**

|  | Biological mothers (*n* = 100) | | Social mothers (*n* = 100) | | t[1] |
|---|---|---|---|---|---|
| **Minority stress** | | | | | |
| *Rejection* | | | | | |
| Experiences of rejection | 1.21 | ( .23) | 1.20 | ( .21) | .29 |
| *Perception of social stigma* | | | | | |
| Expected social stigma | 4.04 | ( .72) | 3.93 | ( .72) | 1.41 |
| Assumed heterosexuals' attitudes | 2.43 | ( .62) | 2.47 | ( .62) | .59 |
| *Internalized homophobia* | | | | | |
| IHP directed to the self | 1.37 | ( .51) | 1.36 | ( .48) | .22 |
| IHP directed to others | 1.89 | ( .67) | 1.95 | ( .67) | -.77 |
| **Parental experience of parenthood** | | | | | |
| Parental burden | 2.03 | ( .78) | 2.05 | ( .81) | -.31 |
| Parental competence | 4.44 | ( .39) | 4.47 | ( .38) | -.80 |
| Parental justification | 1.83 | ( .78) | 1.88 | ( .93) | -.42 |
| **Emotional/ behavioral adjustment of children** | | | | | |
| Internalizing behavioral problems | 5.99 | ( 4.64) | 5.86 | ( 4.17) | .32 |
| Externalizing behavioral problems | 8.15 | ( 6.58) | 8.69 | ( 6.62) | .20 |
| Total behavioral problems | 19.26 | (11.73) | 19.5 | (11.55) | .80 |

[1] Paired t-test

*Experience of parenthood.* There were no significant differences between biological mothers and social mothers on parental competence, parental burden, and parental justification.

*The emotional/ behavioral adjustment of children.* On average children in the present sample were well adjusted. There were no significant differences between biological mothers' report of child emotional/ behavioral adjustment and the social mothers' report.

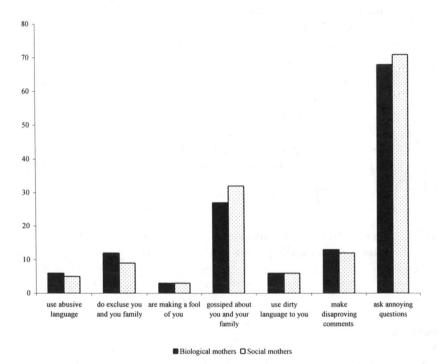

■ Biological mothers ☐ Social mothers

*Figure 6.1* Lesbian mothers' (biological and social) experiences with various forms of rejection

### Minority stress, experience of parenthood, and child adjustment

To assess the relation of the different dimensions of minority stress with parental experience of parenthood and child adjustment, correlation coefficients (Pearson's Product-Moment correlation r) were calculated. Correlations were conducted on the pooled group of lesbian mothers, because biological and social mothers did not differ significantly on minority stress, experiences of parenthood, and child adjustment.

*Minority stress, and experience of parenthood.* As shown in Table 6.2, almost all dimensions of minority stress were significantly correlated with parental justification. Lesbian mothers who reported more experiences of rejection, felt more often pressed to justify the quality of motherhood towards others. Furthermore, lesbian mothers who more strongly agreed that heterosexuals think negatively about homosexuality also felt they had to justify the quality of motherhood more

**Table 6.2  Pearson Product-Moment correlation between Minority stress, Parental experience of parenthood, and Child adjustment**

| | Parental experience of parenthood | | | Child adjustment | | |
| --- | --- | --- | --- | --- | --- | --- |
| | Parental burden | Parental competence | Parental justification | Internalizing behavior problems | Externalizing behavior problems | Total behavior problems |
| Experiences of rejection | .15** | -.13** | .23*** | .15** | .18*** | .21*** |
| Expected social stigma | .04 | -.04 | .09 | .01 | -.02 | .01 |
| Assumed heterosexuals' attitudes | -.01 | -.08 | .24*** | .10 | .03 | .09 |
| IHP directed to the self | .08 | -.09 | .22*** | .03 | -.04 | -.01 |
| IHP directed to others | -.06 | .04 | .14* | -.05 | .01 | -.01 |

*p<.05;  **p<.01;  ***p<.001

often. Mothers with high levels of negative feelings toward their own homosexuality (e.g., IHP towards self) and mothers with high levels of negative feelings towards other lesbian women and gay men also felt they had to justify the quality of their parenthood more often.

In order to examine the unique contribution of the dimensions of minority stress on justification, we conducted a multiple regression analyses. In this analyses, parental justification was the dependent variable. Those dimensions of minority stress related to parental justification were used as predictors, namely rejection, assumed heterosexuals' attitudes, IHP directed to others, and IHP directed to self. Rejection ($\beta$= .17, $p$ < .05), assumptions about straight people's attitudes toward homosexuality ($\beta$= .17, $p$ < .01), and IHP directed to the self ($\beta$= .15, $p$ < .05) were found to make significant and independent contributions to the variance explained in parental justification ($R^2$= .12, $p$ < .001).

There was also a significant correlation between rejection and parental burden. Lesbian mothers who experienced more rejection, also felt more burdened by the child. In addition, rejection was significantly correlated with parental competence. Lesbian mothers who experienced more rejection, also felt less competent as parents. The other aspects of minority stress and parental burden were not related, nor were there significant associations between these other dimensions and parental competence.

*Minority stress and child adjustment.* Table 6.2 also shows correlations between minority stress and the maternal reports of child adjustment. Lesbian mother's experiences with rejection were the only minority stress variable that was significantly related to child adjustment (see Table 6.2). Lesbian mothers who reported more experiences with rejection, reported higher levels of children's externalizing and internalizing behavior problems and also reported higher levels of children's overall problems behavior score. No significant associations were found between the other aspects of minority stress and child adjustment.

## 6.4 Discussion

To explore diversity within lesbian families, the present study examined several dimensions of minority stress, and the relationship of minority stress with experiences of parenthood and child adjustment. The lesbian mothers in this sample generally reported low levels of rejection, perceived stigma, and internalized homophobia. In spite of the low levels of minority stress, higher levels of rejection were, as expected, associated with more experiences of parental stress and more sense to justify the quality of the parent-child relationship. Having negative assumptions about straight people's attitudes toward homosexuality, and having higher levels of internalized homophobia, were also associated with more parental justification. Levels of rejection were associated with more emotional/behavioral problems in children.

Some of the relations we hypothesized to find were not supported by the findings. There is, for example, no support for the view that perceived stigma, and internalized homophobia associated with more parental stress (parental burden and parental incompetence). Lesbian mothers' levels of perceived stigma and internalized homophobia also was not associated with lower adjustment in children. Other aspects that are not related to lesbian parenthood and minority stress, of course, would be more related to parental stress and child adjustment. It has been shown that mothers having high workload, with more children in the family, or mothers who perceive their child as fussy-difficult report more parental stress (Österber & Hagekull, 2000). Such aspects were not included in the present study, because the purpose of the study was to analyze the impact of factors related to minority stress.

Before discussing and interpreting the results, it should be mentioned that the low levels of minority stress experienced by lesbian mothers in the present study, may be explained by the relatively positive climate regarding homosexuality in the Netherlands (Sandfort, 1998; Waaldijk, 1993; Widmer, Treas, & Newcomb, 1998). Lower levels of social acceptance of homosexuality lead to higher levels of rejection, and therefore the observed level of negative treatment might be more pronounced in other Western countries than in the Netherlands. Furthermore, it might be that due to the decision to become a mother within a lesbian relationship, participants in the present study were probably higher in self-acceptance than many others lesbians. Morris, Balsam, and Rothblum (2002), for example, found that lesbians who had children before coming out were more likely to have ever received mental health counseling than those who had children after coming out.

One should also bear in mind that the educational level of participants in this study is relatively high. On the other hand, several studies have shown that lesbian women tend to be more highly educated (Steckel, 1987; McCandlish, 1987; Patterson, 1994; Flaks, Ficher, Masterpasqua, & Joseph, 1995; Sandfort, 1998; Johnson, Wadsworth, Wellings, & Field, 1994). It seems that children from lesbian low-SES mother families are more likely than those from middle-class lesbian mother families to experience peer stigma about issues related to the lesbian identity of the mother (Tasker & Golombok, 1997).

Other studies on minority stress show that experiences with discrimination and violence, are major roadblocks to well being for many lesbians (Garnets, Herek, & Levy, 1990; Herek, Gillis, & Cogan, 1999). Negative reflections from others might be internalized and might lead to uncertainty towards ways to cope with being a mother in a non-traditional family. Garnets et al. (1990) described the psychological mechanism that could explain the effect of discrimination, and violence on well being among lesbian women, that is, victimization interferes with the perception of the world as meaningful and orderly. Lesbian women who have experienced negative treatment, try to restore order to their perception of the world by responding with self-devaluation. This psychological mechanism may also explain the associations between minority stress, especially negative treatment, and parental justification and parental reports of child adjustment. Emotional/ behavioral problems in children may be more determined by factors that are not related at all with growing up in a lesbian family. In several studies it was found that the psychological adjustment of children in planned lesbian families did not differ from that of children in a two-parent heterosexual family (Chan, Raboy, & Patterson, 1998; Golombok, 2001). In our study, however, we investigated differences within planned lesbian families and our results suggests that minority stress indeed may have a negative impact on mothers and children.

From anecdotal stories and interview studies, it is known that the main concerns of lesbian women who are thinking about getting children are the possible negative implications of raising a child in a non-traditional family in a heterosexist and homophobic society (Gartrell et al., 1996; Leiblum, Palmer, & Spector, 1995; Weeks, Heaphy, & Donovan, 2001). Lesbian women are concerned about their children's possible disadvantage in the relationships outside the family caused by the prejudice they will encounter from peers (Touroni & Coyle, 2002). However, research conducted among young adults who grew up in a lesbian mother family in the United Kingdom, has found that as children they were no more likely than the children of a heterosexual mother to have been teased or bullied by peers (Golombok, 2000; Tasker & Golombok, 1997). Vanfraussen et al. (2002) reported that children in lesbian families were not more frequently teased than children in heterosexual families about aspects such clothes, and physical appearance. However, family-related incidents of teasing were only mentioned by children from lesbian families. It would be interesting to examine how the children in planned lesbian families cope with being a member of a minority group.

A limitation to the present study is that some of the scales were used for the first time in a study among lesbian mothers and were not validated for this specific group. Furthermore, since we relied on self-reports, it could be that some measures, such as negative experiences and child adjustment, are affected by a tendency of lesbian mothers to provide socially desirable answers. As a consequence, some of the perceptions of the respondents might not accurately reflect the actual situation. Finally, the design used in this study was cross-sectional, which implies that one has to be cautious in ascribing causal directions to the established relationship.

The present study is one of the first studies on lesbian parenthood to examine relations between minority stress and parental experience of parenthood and child adjustment. It is also the largest study to date on lesbian families. Our findings underscore the importance of the effect of minority stress on the lives of lesbian mothers and their children. Health care providers working with lesbian families, but also teachers having children from lesbian mothers in the classroom, should appraise the effect of minority stress and support coping responses in dealing it.

# VII

# Discussion

Research on lesbian families started about 25 years ago and proceeded in two phases. In the first phase, systematic studies of lesbian families focused on lesbian families with children who born in a previous, heterosexual relationship. These early studies were designed to evaluate judicial presumptions about children's gender development, and the negative consequences for the psychological health and well being of the children in these families. More recently, a handful of studies have included lesbian families whose children were born to the lesbian couple (planned lesbian families). The focus of the study reported on in this thesis was on planned lesbian families. The central aim was to compare these families with heterosexual families on family characteristics (e.g., the desire to have children), parenting behavior (e.g., parental concern), and children's social adjustment (behavior problems). An additional aim was to examine the relation between minority stress (i.e., experiences of rejection) and several family characteristics and child adjustment. This chapter presents and discusses the main findings. It ends with an outline of the limitations of the inquiries conducted and by presenting recommendations for future research.

*Family characteristics*
It was found that, on average, both biological and social lesbian mothers are older than heterosexual parents. Lesbian women start to think about having children at an older age than heterosexuals do, because conception requires a lot of forethought, and donor insemination takes more time than does getting pregnant by natural conception (Botchan et al., 2001).

Lesbian biological and social mothers differ from heterosexual mothers and fathers in that their desire to have a child is stronger and in that they are more engaged with the issue of having children. Lesbian women go through great pains to realize their desire to have a child. They carefully weigh the pros and cons of having children. Concerns that are possibly important in the transition to parenthood may be possible negative implications of raising a child in a non traditional family and the effects this has on children.

After having made the decision to have a child, lesbian couples have to decide on a number of other issued, such as the way conception will take place (i.e., by donor insemination at a fertility-clinic, or self-insemination by donor sperm provided by a friend). Furthermore, new reproductive technologies can be seen as unnatural forms of transition to parenthood. For a lesbian woman, the transition is comparable to the infertility experience of infertile heterosexual couples. These circumstances are associated with an enhanced awareness of the importance of parenthood and of having children (Van Balen & Trimbos-Kemper, 1995; Van Balen, 1996). These aspects may lead to a stronger involvement in parenting.

It seems that the hierarchy of parenthood motives preferred by biological and social lesbian mothers is similar to that preferred by heterosexual parents. Feelings of affection and expectations that parenthood will provide fulfillment are at the top of the hierarchy. In Western societies, motives for having children are related to personal fulfillment and emphasize the uniqueness of the parent-child relationship. Feelings of pressure from the environment are at the bottom of the hierarchy. This is in line with the fact that in today's Western societies, parenthood motives are unrelated to social pressure (Van Balen & Inhorn, 2002). Although the order of motives is quite similar, lesbian mothers and heterosexual parents differ in the importance they ascribe to the motives. For example, happiness is more important to biological and social lesbian mothers than it is to heterosexual mothers and fathers, while parenthood identity is less important. This can be explained by the fact that in lesbian mothers happiness is more explicit and manifest because it takes a lot of effort to realize the desire to have a child. That parenthood identity is less important may be because the items on the identity scale refer to the desire to have children as a means of achieving adulthood and strengthening one's identity. For lesbian women, however, the integration of their lesbian identity into a positive understanding of self is the way of achieving adulthood.

Lesbian social mothers spend more time on family tasks and less time on professional employment than heterosexual fathers do. Perhaps the absence of gender polarization in lesbian families leads to more equal burden-sharing in the family. Evolutionary theorists assume that males are more likely to invest less in their children than females, because males are confident that females will continue to invest in their children even if it is little (Bjorklund, Yunger, & Pellegrini, 2002). With respect to employment outside the home, it may be that lesbian partners understand each other's career opportunities and challenges better than partners in a heterosexual relationship do (Dunne, 1998). Perhaps this is due to the fact that lesbian women would like to have an independent position as provider in a relationship (Sandfort & Bos, 1998; Schuyf, 1994).

Lesbian social mothers feel more pressured to justify the quality of parenthood than heterosexual fathers do. Possibly this is related to the absence of a biological tie with the children, which drives them to do their utmost to be a 'good mom.' Like adoptive parents, social mothers may face difficulties in developing an adequate sense of acting as a full parent (Grotevant & Kohler, 1999). It is also likely that lesbian social mothers feel pressured to be visible as a mother (De Kanter, 1996; Muzio, 1999, Nekkebroeck & Brewaeys, 2002), because they think that their position is different from that of lesbian and heterosexual biological parents. Other studies (e.g., Gartrell et al., 1999) have shown that although social mothers consider themselves to be equal parents, they display feelings of jealousy and competitiveness concerning child rearing issues. Social mothers indicate that, in their view, the biological tie is an important factor affecting mother-child attachment. This perhaps explains why lesbian social mothers report a high level of parental justification.

Both lesbian biological and social mothers depart from less traditional in child rearing goals than heterosexual mothers and fathers. These findings are in line with those of Tasker and Golombok (1997) regarding the way lesbian and heterosexual parents discuss sexuality with their children. Lesbian mothers feel more comfortable discussing this issue than heterosexual parents do. Teenage children in lesbian families communicate feelings on sexuality to their parents more openly.

*Parental behavior*

Social mothers display more emotional involvement, parental concern, induction, and respect for the child's autonomy than heterosexual fathers do. On the other hand, lesbian social mothers less often use power assertion, structure and limit setting compared to heterosexual fathers. Such differences are considered to be a reflection of a gender effect. Women are supposed to be more expressive, nurturant, and sensitive, while men exhibit instrumental competence more often (Chodorow, 1978; Gilligan, 1982; Parson & Bales, 1955; Lamb, 1999). Contrary to these expectations, in our study four (emotional concern, parental concern, induction, structure and limit setting) of the six observed differences in parental behavior between lesbian social mothers and heterosexual fathers disappeared after controlling for family characteristics. What mediated the observed differences in parental behavior were parental justification, intensity of desire, and Employment-Family Time Index. Lesbian social mothers differ from heterosexual fathers not only on gender, but also on two other important aspects. The position of lesbian social mothers does not fit into the larger societal definition of what constitutes a family (de Kanter, 1996; Muzio, 1999, Nekkebroeck & Brewaeys, 2002), and lesbian social mothers lack a genetic link with the child. To compensate for this, lesbian social mothers tend to be highly emotionally involved in child rearing.

*Child development*

Findings based on the Child Behavior Checklist (CBCL/4-18, Achenbach, 1991; Verhulst, van den Ende, & Koot, 1996) indicate that children in lesbian families generally function as well as children in heterosexual families do. Given the greater emotional involvement of lesbian social mothers in parenting, it could be expected that children brought up in lesbian families would score well above average. However, this was not found. This result is in line with the supposition of Roberts and Strayer (1987): higher levels of warmth and parental involvement do not result in the child's even greater well being once a certain threshold has been passed. This was also found in studies among other parents who also have go through great lengths before they could fulfill their wish to create a family, such as IVF, AID, and adoptive parents (Golomok et al., 1995; Van Balen, 1998).

*Minority stress*
Biological and social lesbian mothers report low levels of rejection, perceive little stigmatization, and manifest low levels of internalized homophobia (IHP). However, minority stress is significantly related to experiences of parenthood. Lesbian mothers who experience rejection feel more burdened with child rearing and less competent, and they defend their position as a mother more strongly (parental justification). Lesbian mothers with higher levels of perceived stigma and IHP feel significantly more often that they have to defend their position as a mother. Finally, mothers who feel rejected are more likely to report behavioral problems in their children. Several authors (Gillespie, 1999; Nelson, 1996; Stacey & Bilarz, 2001) state that homophobia and discrimination are the main reasons why parental sexual orientation matters at all as regards parental behavior and child adjustment.

*Limitations*
The study presented in this thesis had some limitations. First, there is the issue of representativeness. It is not entirely clear whether the lesbian mothers involved in the study are representative of planned lesbian families in general in the Netherlands. Second, some of the instruments used have not yet been validated (e.g., parental justification scale), or were not validated for the specific group of lesbian mothers (e.g., minority stress scales). Third, it was found that lesbian social mothers and heterosexual fathers differ on several aspects of family characteristics and parental behavior. However, due to the design of the study (i.e., a comparison between planned lesbian families and heterosexual families), it is unclear whether these differences can be attributed to gender, the absence of a genetic tie with the child, less favorable attitudes toward homosexuality and lesbian families in our society, or a combination of these aspects.

*Recommendations for future research*
Research on child rearing in planned lesbian families and on the development of children in these families offer opportunities to assess the necessity of rearing children in families with a father and a mother. However, as mentioned above some issues related to unraveling the inference of gender, a genetic link, and minority status remain unanswered. Therefore, research with another design than used in the present study should be initiated. A comparison, for example between, planned lesbian families, heterosexual families and two gay fathers and/or families headed by a gay father(s) and a lesbian mother(s), could help to unravel the confounding of possible influences of gender and genetic link. Researchers could also conduct experiments wherein a child is observed in interaction with his/her parent and in interaction with another adult. Parents and adults should be matched on gender, sexual orientation and parenthood status. Such a design would allow for a comparison between lesbian parents and non-parents, and heterosexual parents and non-parents, and offer the opportunity for testing assumptions about links between gender and genetic tie, and child rearing behavior.

No differences were found between the children of lesbian parents and those of heterosexual parents on psychological adjustment. The children in our study were between four and eight years old, and at this stage of development a child's well being is largely under the influence of the family context. As children grow older, the importance of friends and peers increases (Bukowski, Sippola, & Hoza, 1999; Erickson, 1968; Mrug, Hoza, & Bukowski, 2004). This makes them increasingly aware of their non traditional family situation compared to that of peers. In a follow-up study one should also focus on these aspect were planned lesbian families are confronted with in other developmental stages of their family history.

In may be that some of the children involved in the present study, in the future have to cope with homophobic teasing and bullying from classmates. Therefore, it is important to examine how parents and children cope to different negative reactions of surroundings (minority stress), and whether it influences their adjustment. This is an import issue for future reseach, because recent publications have shown that the acceptance of homosexuality in schools is decreasing dramatically (NVIH/COC, 2003; de Graaf, Van De Meerendonk, Veenix, & Vanwesenbeeck, 2003).

# References

Abidin, R. R. (1983). *Parenting stress index: Manual*. Charlottesville: Pediatric Psychology Press.

Achenbach, T.M. (1991). *Manual for the child behavior checklist/ 4-18*. Burlington, VT: University of Verment Department of Psychiatry.

Arditti, R., Klein, R. D. & Minden, S. (Eds.), (1989). *Test-tube women: What future for mother hood?* London: Houghton Mifflin.

Ås, D. (1978). Studies of time use: problems and prospects. *Acta Sociologica, 2*, 125-141.

Baumrind, D. (1989). Rearing competent children. In W. Damon (Ed.), *Child development today and tomorrow* (pp. 349-378). Burlington: University of Vermont Department of Psychiatry.

Benedek, Th. (1970a). The family as a psychological field. In E. J. Anthony & Th. Benedek (Eds.), *Parenthood, its psychology and psychopathology* (pp. 109-136). Boston: Little, Brown & Co.

Benedek, Th. (1970b). Fatherhood and providing. In E. J. Anthony & Th. Benedek (Eds.), *Parenthood, its psychology and psychopathology* (pp. 195-200). Boston: Little, Brown & Co.

Bjorklund, D.F., Yunger, J.L. & Pellegrini, A.D. (2002). The Evolution of Parenting and Evolutionary Approaches to Childrearing. In M.H. Bornstein (Ed.), *Handbook of parenting: Vol. 2. Biology and Ecology of Parenting* (pp. 3-30). Mahwah, NJ: Erlbaum Associates Publisher.

Blankenhorn, D. (1995). *Fatherless America: Confronting our most urgent social problem*. New York: Basic.

Block, J. H. (1965). *The child rearing practices report*. Berkeley, CA: University of California, Institute of human development.

Blumenfeld, W. J. & Raymond, D. (1988). *Looking at gay and lesbian life*. Boston: Beacon.

Blumstein, P. & Schwartz, P. (1983). *American couples*. New York: William Morrow.

Bonsel, G. J. & Van Der Maas, P. J. (1994). *Aan de wieg van de toekomst; Scenario's voor de zorg rondom de menselijke voortplanting 1995-2010 [At the birthplace of the future; Scripts for human reproduction care 1995-2010]*. Houten/ Diegem: Bohn Staflue Van Loghum.

Bos, H. & Sandfort, Th. G. M. (1999). *Homoseksuele mannen en vrouwen over hun werksituatie. 'De prijs die ik betaal' [Gay men and lesbian women about their workplac. The prize I pay for]*. Zoetermeer: ABVAKABO FNV.

Bos, H. M. W., Van Balen, F. & Van Den Boom, D. C. (2003). Planned lesbian families: their desire and motivation to have children. *Human Reproduction, 18*, 2216-2224.

Botchan, A., Hauser, R., Gamzu, R., Yogev, L., Paz, G. & Yavetz, H. (2001). Results of 6139 artificial insemination cycles with donor spermatozoa. *Human Reproduction, 16*, 2298-2304.

Brewaeys, A., Ponjaert-Kristoffersen, I., Van Steirteghm, A. C. & Devroey, P. (1993). Children from anonymous donors: An inquiry into homosexual and heterosexual parents' attitudes. *Journal of Psychosomatic Obstetrics and Gynaecology, 14*, 23-35.

Brewaeys, A., Devroey, P., Helmerhorst, F.M., Van Hall, E.V. & Ponjaert, I. (1995). Lesbian mothers who conceived after donor insemination: a follow-up study. *Human Reproduction, 10*, 2731-2735.

Brewaeys, A., Ponjaert, I., Van Hall, E. V. & Golombok, S. (1997). Donor insemination: child development & family functioning in lesbian mother families with 4 to 8 year old children. *Human Reproduction, 12*, 1349-1359.

Brinkman, J. (2000) *De vragenlijst [A Questionnaire]*. Groningen: Wolter-Noordhoff.

Brooks, V. (1981). *Minority stress and lesbian women*. Lexington, MA: Lexington Books, D.C. Health and Co.

Bukowski, W.M., Sippola, L. K. & Hoza, B. (1999). Same and other: Interdependency between participation in same- and other-sex friendships. *Journal of Youth and Adolescence, 28*, 439-459

Bussey, K. & Bandura, A. (1999). Social cognitive theory of gender development and differentiation. *Psychological Review, 106*, 676-713.

Cameron, P. & Cameron, K. (1996). Homosexual parents. *Adolescence, 31*, 757-776.

Cameron, P., Cameron, K. & Landess, T. (1996). Errors by the American psychiatric association,
the American psychiatric association, and the national educational association in representing
homosexuality in amicus briefs about amendment 2 to the U.S. supreme court. *Psychological
Reports, 79*, 383-404.

CBS (1999). *De mobiliteit van de Nederlandse bevolking, 1997, deel 3: tijdsbesteding en
maatschappelijke participatie [Mobility of the Dutch population, 1997. part III: The use of
time and participation in society].* Voorburg/ Heerlen: CBS.

Chan, R. W., Brooks, R. C., Raboy, B. & Patterson, C. J. (1998). Division of labor among lesbian
and heterosexual parents: Associations with children's adjustment. *Journal of Family Psychology, 12*, 402-419.

Chan, R. W., Raboy, B. & Patterson, C. J. (1998). Psychosocial adjustment among children conceived via donor insemination by lesbian and heterosexual mothers. *Child Development, 69*,
443-457.

Chodorow, N. (1978). *The reproduction of mothering: Psychoanalysis and the sociology of gender.* Berkeley, CA: University of California Press.

Clarke, V. (2002). Sameness and differences in research on lesbian parenting. *Journal of Community and Applied Social Psychology, 12*, 210-222.

Cochran, M. & Niegro, S. (1995). Parenting and social networks. In M. H. Bornstein (Ed.), *Handbook of parenting: Vol. 3. Status and social conditions of parenting* (pp. 393-418). Mahwah,
N.J: Erlbaum.

Colpin, H. (1994). *Het opvoeden van een kind na medisch begeleide bevruchting, theoretische en
empirische exploratie [Raising children following medically assisted reproduction, theoretical
and empirical exploration.* Leuven: Katholieke Universiteit Leuven.

Colpin, H., de Munter, A. & Vandemeulebroecke, L. (1998). Parenthood motives in IVF-mothers.
*Journal of Psychosomatic Obstetrics and Gynaecology, 19*, 19-27.

Commissie Gelijke Behandeling [Equal treatment committee] (2000). *Onderzoek uit eigen beweg-
ing [Research of one's own movement].* Utrecht: CGB.

Corea, G. (1985). *The mother machine, reproductive technology from artificial insemination to
artificial wombs.* New York: Harper and Row.

Crespi, L. (2001). And baby makes three: A dynamic look at development and conflict in lesbian
families. In D.F. Glazer & J. Drescher (Eds.), *Gay and lesbian parenting* (pp. 7-30). London:
The Haworth Press.

Crnic, K. A., Greenberg, M.T., Ragozin, A.S., Robinson, M.M. & Basham, R.B. (1983). Effects of
stress and social support on mothers and premature and full-term infants. *Child Development,
54*, 209-217.

De Graaf, H. & Sandfort, Th. (2001). *De maatschappelijke positie van homoseksuele mannen en
lesbische vrouwen [The position of gay men and lesbian women in society].* Utrecht: RNG.

De Graaf, H., Van De Meerendonk, B., Vennix, P. & Vanwesenbeeck, I. (2003). Beter voor de klas,
beter voor de school. Werkbeleving en gezondheid van homo-en biseksuele mannen en
vrouwen in het onderwijs *[Work experience and health of homosexual and bisexual men and
women working in the field of education]* Utrecht: RNG.

De Kanter, R. (1996). *Een vader is een mannelijke moeder, eigenlijk. De geslachtsidentiteit van
kinderen in verschillende leefvormen [In fact a father is a masculine mother. Gender identity
of children in several family types].* Utrecht: J. Van Arkel.

De Leeuw, E. & De Heer, W. (2002). Trends in household Survey non-response: A longitudinal
and international comparison. In R.M. Groves, D.A., Dillman, J.L. & R.J.A. Little (Eds.),
*Survey non-response* (pp. 41-54). New York: Willey.

Dekovic, M., Gerrits, L. A. W., Groenendaal, J. H. A. & Noom, M. J. (1996). *Bronnen van opvoedingsondersteuning, inventarisatie (BOO) [Questionnaire for the measurement of support with
respect to child rearing practices].* Utrecht: Universiteit van Utrecht.

DiPlacido, J. (1998). Minority stress among lesbians, gay men, and bisexuals: A consequence of
heterosexism, homophobia, and stigmatization. In G. M. Herek (Ed.), *Stigma and sexual orientation. Understanding prejudice against lesbians, gay men, and bisexuals: Psychological
perspectives on lesbian and gay issues, vol. 4* (pp.138-159). Thousand Oaks, CA: Sage.

Dunne, G.A. (1998). Pioneers behind our own front doors: New models for the organization of work in domestic partnerships. *Work, Employment and Society, 12,* 273-296.

Dunne, G.A. (2000). Opting into motherhood: Lesbian blurring the boundaries and transforming the meaning of parenthood and kinship. *Gender and Society, 14,* 11-35.

Erickson, E. (1968). *Identity: youth and crisis.* New York: Norton.

Erickson, M. F., Sroufe, L. A. & Egeland, B. (1985). The relationship beyween quality of attachment and behavior problems in preschool in a high-risk sample. In I. Bretherton & E. Waters (Eds.), *Growing points of attachment: Theory and reserach. Monographs of the society for reserach in child development, Vol. 50* (pp. 147- 166). Chicago: The Univeristy of Chicago Press.

Fawcett, J. T. (1972). Introduction and summary of workshop discussions and conclusions. In J.T. Fawcett (Ed.), *The satisfaction and costs of children: Theories, concepts, and methods* (pp. 1-10). Honolulu: East-West Centre Population Institute.

Fawcett, J. T., Albores, S. & Arnold, F. S. (1972). The value of children among ethnic groups in Hawaii: exploratory measurement. In J.T. Fawcett (Ed.), *The satisfaction and costs of children: Theories, concepts, and methods* (pp. 234-259). Honolulu: East-West Centre Population Institute.

Fawcett, J. T. (1978). The value and cost of the first child. In W.B. Miller & L.F. Newman (Eds.), *The first child and family formation* (pp. 244-265). Chapel Hill: University of North Carolina.

Flaks, D. K., Ficher, I. Masterpasqua, F. & Joseph, G. (1995). Lesbian choosing motherhood: A comparative study of lesbian and heterosexual parents and their children. *Developmental Psychology, 31,* 105-114.

Kaiser Family Foundation (2001). *Inside- out: A report on the experience of lesbians, gays, and bisexuals in America and the public's views on issues and policies related to sexual orientation.* Menlo Park: The Henrey J. Kaiser Family Foundation.

Furstenberg, F.F. & Cherlin, A.J. (1991). *Divided Families.* Cambridge, M.A: Harvard University Press.

Garnets, L., Herek, G.M. & Levy, B. (1990). Violence and victimization of lesbians and gay men: Mental health consequences. *Journal of Interpersonal Violence, 5,* 366-383.

Gartrell, N., Hamilton, J., Banks, A., Mosbacher, D., Reed, N., Sparks, C. H. & Bishop, H. (1996). The National lesbian family study; Interviews with prospective mothers. *American Journal of Orthopsychiatry, 66,* 272-281.

Gartrell, N., Banks, A., Reed, N., Hamilton, J., Rodas, C. & Deck, A. (1999). The national lesbian family study: 2. Interviews with mothers of toddlers. *American Journal of Orthopsychiatry, 69,* 362-369.

Gartrell, N., Banks, A., Reed, N., Hamilton, J., Rodas, C. & Deck, A. (2000). The national lesbian family study: 3. Interviews with mothers of five years olds. *American Journal of Orthopsychiatry, 70,* 542-548.

Gerris, J. R. M. , Vermulst, A. A., Boxtel, D. A. A. M., Janssens, J. M. A. M., Zutphen, R. A. H., Van & Felling, A. J. A. (1993). *Child rearing and family in the Netherlands.* Nijmegen: ITS.

Gerrits, L. A. W., Dekovic, M., Groenendaal, J. H. A. & Noom, M. J. (1996). Opvoedings-gedrag. In J. Rispens, J. M. A. Hermanns & W. H. J. Meeus (Eds.), *Opvoeden in Nederland [Child rearing in the Netherlands].* Assen: Van Gorcum.

Gerrits, L. A. W. (2000). *Parenting: Father-mother comparison and the validity of self- reported parenting behavior.* Utrecht: Utrecht University Press.

Gershon, T.D., Tschann, J.M. & Jemerin, J.H. (1999). Stigmatization, self-esteem, and coping among the adolescent children of lesbian mothers. *Journal of Adolescent Health, 24,* 437-445.

Gerson, J. M. (1983). A scale of motivation of parenthood: index of parenthood motivation. *Journal of Psychology, 113,* 211-220.

Giddens, A. (1992). *The transformation of intimacy: Sexuality, love and eroticism in modern societies.* Standford, C.A.: Stanford University Press.

Gillespie, P. (1999). Preface. In G. Kaeser & P. Gillespie (Eds.), *Love makes a family: Portraits of lesbian, gay, bisexual, and transgender parents and their families* (pp. xi-xviii). Amherst, MA: University of Massachusetts Press.

Gilligan, C. (1982). *In a different voice: Psychological theory and women's development.* Cambridge, MA: Harvard University Press.

Goffman, E. (1963). *Stigma: Notes on the management of spoiled identity.* New York: Simon and

Schuster.

Golombok, S., Spencer, A. & Rutter, M. (1983). Children in lesbian and single parent households: psychosexual and psychiatric appraisal. *Journal of Child Psychology and Psychiatry, 24,* 551-572.

Golombok, S. (1992). Psychological functioning in infertility patients. *Human Reproduction, 7,* 208-298.

Golombok, S., Cook, R., Bish, A. & Murray, C. (1995). Families created by the new reproductive technologies: Quality of parenting and social and emotional development of the children. *Child Development, 66,* 285-298.

Golombok, S. & Tasker, F. L. (1996). Do parents influence the sexual orientation of their children? Findings from a longitudinal study of lesbian families. *Developmental Psychology, 32,* 3-11.

Golombok, S. Tasker. F. L. & Murray, C. (1997). Children raised in fatherless families from infancy: Family relationships and the socio-emotional development of children of lesbian and single heterosexual mothers. *Journal of Child Psychology and Psychiatry, 38,* 783-791.

R— Golombok, S. (2000). *Parenting: What really counts?* New York, NY: Routledge.

Golombok, S., Perry, B., Burston, A., Murray, C., Mooney-Somers, J., Stevens, M. & Golding, J. (2003). Children with lesbian parents: A community study. *Developmental Psychology, 39,* 20-33.

Goodnow, J.J. & Collins, W.A. (1990). Development according to parents. The nature, success, and consequences of parents' ideas. Hillsdale: Laurence Erlbaum Associates, Publishers.

Gottman, J. & Sussman, M. (1990). Children of gay and lesbian parents. In F. Bozett & M. Sussman (Eds.), *Homosexuality and family relations* (pp. 177-196). New York, Harrington Park.

Green, R. (1978). Sexual identity of 37 children raised by homosexual or transsexual parents. *American Journal Psychiatry, 135,* 692-697.

Green, R., Mandel, J., Hotveld, M., Gray, J. & Smith, L (1986). Lesbian mothers and their children: A comparison with solo parent heterosexual mothers and their children. *Archives of Sexual Behavior, 15,* 167-184.

Groenendaal, J. H. A., Dekovic, M. & Noom, M.J. (1996). Gezinskenmerken [Family characteristics]. In J. Rispens, J. M. A. Hermanns & W. H. J. Meeus (Eds.), *Opvoeden in Nederland [Child rearing in the Netherlands]* (pp. 95-113). Assen: Van Gorcum.

Grotevant, H. D. & Kohler, J. K. (1999). Adoptive families. In M. E. Lamb (Ed.), *Parenting and child development in 'nontraditional families'* (pp. 161–190). Mahwah, NJ: Erlbaum.

Grusec, J. E., Rudy, D. & Martini, T. (1997). Parenting cognitions and child outcomes: An overview and implications for children's internalization of values. A handbook of contemporary theory. In J. E. Grusec & L. Kuczynski (Eds.), *Parenting and children's internalization of values* (pp. 259-282). New York: Wiley.

Hammer, J. (1984). A womb of one's own. In R. Arditti, R. Duelli Klein & S. Minden (Eds.), *Test-tube women: What future for motherhood?* (pp. 438-448). London: Pandora Press.

Hare, J. & Richards, L.(1993). Children raised by lesbian couples: Does the context of birth affect father and partner involvement? *Family Relations, 42,* 249-255.

Harne, L. (1997). *Rights of women. Valued families: The lesbian mothers' legal handbook.* London, The women's press.

Harris, M. B. & Turner, P. H. (1985). Gay and lesbian parents. *Journal of Homosexuality, 12,* 101-113.

Herek, G.M., Kimmel, D.C., Amaro, H. & Melton, G.B. (1991). Avoiding heterosexist bias in psychological research. *American Journal of Psychology, 46,* 957-963.

Herek, G.M. & Glunt, E.K. (1995). Identity and community among gay and bisexual men in the AIDS era: Prelimary findings from the Sacramento men's health study. In G.M. Herek & B. Green (Eds.), *AIDS, identity, and community* (pp. 55-84). Thousand Oaks: Sage.

Herek, G.M., Cogan, J.C., Gillis, J.R. & Glunt, E.K. (1997). Correlates of internalized homophobia in a community samples of lesbians and gay men. *Journal of the Gay and Lesbian Medical Association, 2,* 17-25.

Herek, G. M., Gillis, J.R. & Cogan, J.C. (1999). Psychological sequel of hate- crime victimization among lesbian, gay, and bisexual adults. *Journal of Consulting and Clinical Psychology, 67,* 945- 951.

Hoeffer, B. (1981). Children's acquisition of sex-role behavior in lesbian-mother families. *American Journal of Orthopsychiatry, 5,* 536-544.

Hoffman, L. W. (1972). A psychological perspective on the value of children to parents: concepts and measures. In J. T. Fawcett (Ed.), *The satisfaction and costs of children: Theories, Concepts, and Methods* (pp. 27-56). Honolulu: East-West Centre Population Institute.

Hoffman, L. W. & Hoffman, M. L. (1973). The Value of Children to Parents. In J.T. Fawcett (Ed.), *Psychological perspectives on population* (pp. 19-76). New York: Basic Books.

Hoffman, L. W. & Manis, D. B. (1979). The value of children in the United States: A new approach to the study of fertility. *Journal of Marriage and the Family, 49*, 583-596.

Hotveld, M. & Mandel, J. (1982). Children of lesbian mothers. In P. W. Weinrich, J. Gonsiorek & M. Hotveld. *Homosexuality: Social, psychological and biological issues* (pp.275-285). Beverly Hills: Sage.

Hubert, A. B. (1996). *Pestgedrag op de werkplek: een exploratief onderzoek. [Mobbing on the workplace].* Leiden: Rijksuniversiteit.

Huggins, S. A. (1989). A comparative study of self esteem of adolescent children of divorced lesbian mothers and divorced heterosexual mothers. In F. Bozett (Ed.), *Homosexuality and family relations* (pp. 177 196). New York: Harrington Park.

Inglehart, R. (1990). *Culture shift in advanced industrial society.* Princeton, N.J.: Princeton University Press.

Jacob, M. C., Klock, S. C. & Maier, D. (1999). Lesbian couples as therapeutic donor insemination recipients: Do they differ from other patients? *Journal of Psychosomatic Obstetrics and Gynecology, 20*, 203-215.

Javaid, G. A. (1993). The children of homosexual and heterosexual single mothers. *Child Psychiatry and Human Development, 23*, 235-248.

Johnson, A. M., Wadsworth, J., Wellings, K. & Field, J. (Eds.)(1994). *Sexual attitudes and lifestyles.* Oxford: Blackwell Scientific.

Kaeser, P. & Gillespie, G. (1999). *Loves makes a family. Portraits of lesbian, gay, bisexual, and transgender parents and their families.* Amherst: University of Massachusetts Press.

Kalfs, P. T. A. M. (1993). *Hour by hour. Effects of the data collection mode in time use research.* Amsterdam: NIMMO.

King, B. R. & Black, N. R. (1999). College students' perceptual stigmatization of the children of lesbian mothers. *American Journal of Orthopsychiatry, 69*, 220-227.

Kirkpatrick, M., Smith, C. & Roy, P. (1981). Lesbian mothers and their children: A comparative survey. *American Journal of Orthopsychiatry, 51*, 545-51.

Knight, R.H. (1997). Homosexual parents are not in a child's best interests. In T.L. Roleff (Ed.), *Gay rights* (pp. 84-89). San Diego, CA: Greenhaven Press.

Knijn, T. (1986) Motivatie voor moeder- en vaderschap. In Engelen, P. (Ed*.), Ouderschap in verandering [Changes in parenthood]*(pp. 43-55). Lisse: Swets and Zeitlinger.

Kochanska, G., Kuzynski, L. & Radke- Yarrow, M. (1989). Correspondence between mother's self-reported and observed child rearing practices. *Child Development, 60*, 56-63.

Koepke, L., Hare, J. & Moran, P.B. (1992). Relationship quality in a sample of lesbian couples with children and child-free lesbian couples. *Family Relations, 41*, 224-229.

Kurdek, L. A. (2001). Differences between heterosexual non-parent couples and gay, lesbian, and heterosexual parent couples. *Journal of Family Issues, 6*, 727-754.

Lamb, M. E. (1999). Parental behavior, family processes, and child development in non-traditional and traditionally understudied families. In M .E. Lamb (Ed), *Parenting and child development in 'non- traditional families'* (pp.1-14). London: Lawrence Erlbaum associates, publishers.

Langdridge, D., Connoly, K. & Sheeran, P. (2000). Reasons for wanting a child: A network analytic study. *Journal of Reproductive and Infant Psychology, 18*, 321-338.

Latten, J. & Cuijvers, P. F. (1994). *Relatie en gezinsvorming in de jaren negentig [Relationships and family planning in the nineties].* Den Haag: CBS/NGR.

Leiblum, S. R., Palmer, M. G. & Spector, I. P. (1995). Non-traditional mothers: Single heterosexual/lesbian women and lesbian couples electing motherhood via donor insemination. *Journal of Psychosomatic Obstetrics and Gynaecology, 16*, 11-20.

Leymann, H. (1990). Mobbing and psychological terror at workplaces. *Violence and Victims, 5*, 119-126.

Levy, D. M. (1970). The concept of maternal overprotection. In E. J. Anthony & Th. Benedek (Eds.) *Parenthood, its psychology and psychopathology* (pp. 387-410). Boston: Little & Co.

Levy, E. (1989). Lesbian motherhood: identity and social support. *Afflicatia, 4*, 40-53.

Levy, Jr. M.J. (1992). *Maternal influence, the search for social universals*. New Brunswick NJ: Transaction.

Lewin, E. & Lyons, T.A. (1982). Everything in its place. The coexistence of lesbianism and motherhood. In W. Paul, J. D. Weinrich, J. C. Gonsiorek & M. E. Hotveldt (Eds.), *Homosexuality: Social, psychological and biological issues* (pp.249-273). Beverly Hills: Sage.

Lewin, E. (1993). *Lesbian mothers: Accounts of gender in American culture*. Ithaca, NY: Cornell University Press.

Lewis, K. G. (1980). Children of lesbians: their point of view. *Social Work, 25*, 198-203.

Lott-Whitehead, L. & Tully, C.T. (1993). The family lives of lesbian mothers. *Smith College Studies in Social Work, 63*, 265-280.

Maccoby, E.E. & Martin, J.A. (1983). Socialization in the context of the family: Parent-child interaction. In P. H. Mussen (Ed.), *Handbook of child psychology: Vol. 4. Socialization, personality, and social development* (pp. 1-101). New York: Wiley.

Maccoby, E.E. (2000). Parenting and its effects on children: On reading and misreading behavior genetics. *Annual Review of Psychology, 51*, 1-27.

Mays, V.M. & Cochran, S.D. (2001). Mental health correlates of perceived discrimination among lesbian, gay, and bisexual adults in the United states. *American Journal of Public Health, 91*, 1869-1876.

Maxwell, N. G. (2001). Opening civil marriage to same-gender couples: a Netherlands- United States comparison., *Electronic Journal of Comparative Law*, 4.3. Retrieved April 23, 2001, from the World Wide Web: http://law.kub.nl/ejcl/43/ art43-1.html.

McCandlish, B. M. (1987). Against all odds: Lesbian mothers family dynamics. Gay and lesbian parents. In F. Bozett (Ed.), *Homosexuality and family relations* (pp. 23-36). New York: Harrington Park

Meyer, J. (1989). Gues who's coming to dinner this time? A study of gay intimate relationships and the support for those relationships. *Marriage and Family Review, 14*, 59-82.

Meyer, I.H. (1995). Minority stress and mental health in gay men. *Journal of Health and Social Behavior, 36*, 38-56.

Meyer, I.H. (2003a). Prejudice, social stress, and mental health in lesbian, gay, and bisexual populations: conceptual issues and research evidence. *Psychological Bulletin, 129*, 674-697.

Meyer, I. H. (2003b). Prejudice as stress: Conceptual and measurement problems. *American Journal of Public Health, 93*, 262-265.

Meyers, S. A. (1999). Mothering in context: Ecological determinants of parent behavior. *Merrill Palmer Quarterly, 45*, 332-357.

Miller, J.A., Jacobsen, R.B. & Bigner, J.J. (1981). The child's home environment for lesbian versus heterosexual mothers: A neglected area of research. *Journal of Homosexuality, 7*, 49-56.

Money, J. & Ehrhardt, A.A. (1972). *Man and women, boy and girl: The differentiation and dimorphism of gender identity from conception to maturity*. Baltimore: John Hopkins University Press.

More, J. & Rochlen, A.B. (1999). Measuring attitudes regarding bisexuality in lesbian, gay male, and heterosexual populations. *Journal of Counseling Psychology, 46*, 353-369.

Morningstar, B. (1999). Lesbian parents: Understanding development pathways. In J. Laird, (Ed.), *Lesbians and lesbian families. Reflection on theory and practice* (pp. 213- 241). New York: Columbia University Press.

Morell, C. M. (1994). *Unwomanly conduct: The challenges of intentional childlessness*. London: Virago.

Morris, J. F., Balsam, K. F. & Rothblum, E.D. (2002). Lesbian and bisexual mothers and non-mothers: Demographics and the coming-out process. *Journal of Family Psychology, 16*, 144-156.

Mrug, S., Hoza, B. & Bukowski, W. (2004). Choosing or being chosen by aggressive disruptive peers: Do they contribute to children's externalizing and internalizing problems? *Journal of Abnormal Child Psychology, 32*, 53-65.

Mucklow, B. & Phelan, G. (1979). Lesbian and traditional mothers' responses to child behavior and self- concept. *Psychological Report, 44*, 880-882.

Muzio, C. (1999). Lesbian co-parenting: On being/being with the invisible (m)other. In J. Laird, (Ed.), *Lesbians and lesbian families. Reflection on theory and practice* (pp. 197- 211). New York: Columbia University Press.

Nelson, F. (1996). *Lesbian motherhood: An exploration of Canadian lesbian families*. Toronto: University Press.

Nekkebroeck, J. & Brewaeys, A. (2002). Lesbische moeders en heteroseksuele ouders, hun rol bekeken vanuit het kindperspectief [Lesbian mothers and heterosexual parents, parenting roles identified from the child's perspective]. *Tijdschrift voor Seksuologie, 26*, 125-130.

Nungesser, L.G. (1983). *Homosexual acts, actors, and identities*. New York: Praeger.

NVIH/COC (2003). *Alle potten en flikker de klas uit [All dykes and faggots out of the classroom]*. Amsterdam: NVIH/COC.

O' Connell, A. (1993). Voices from the heart: The developmental impact of a mother's lesbianism on her adolescent children. *Smith College Studies in Social Work, 63*, 281-299.

Östberg, M. & Hagekull, B. (2000). A structural modelling approach to the understanding of parenting stress. *Journal of Clinical Child Psychology, 29*, 615- 625.

Parke, R. D. (2004). Developmental family. *Annual Review of Psychology, 55*, 365-399.

Parsons T. & Bales R.F. (1956). *Family: Socialisation and interaction process*. London: Routledge & Kegan Paul.

Patterson, C. J. (1992). Children of lesbian and gay parents. *Child Development, 63*, 1025- 1042.

Patterson, C.J. (1994). Children of the lesbian baby boom: Behavioral adjustment, self-concepts, and sex-role identity. In B. Greene & G. Herek (Eds.), *Psychological perspectives on lesbian and gay issues: Vol. 1. Lesbian and gay psychology: Theory, research, and clinical applications* (pp. 156-175). Thousand Oaks, CA: Sage.

Patterson, C.J. (1995a). Lesbian and Gay Parenthood. In M. H. Bornstein (Ed.), *Handbook of Parenting: Vol. 4. Applied and practical parenting* (pp. 255-274). Mahwah, N.J: Erlbaum.

Patterson, C. J. (1995b). Families of the baby boom: Parents' division of labor and children's adjustment. *Developmental Psychology, 31*, 115-123.

Patterson, C.J., & Chan, R. (1999). Families headed by lesbian and gay parents. In M. E. Lamb (Ed.), *Parenting and child development in 'non-traditional families'* (pp.191-219). Mahwah: Lawrence Erlbaum Associates.

Patterson, C. J., & Friel, L. V. (2000). Sexual orientation and fertility. In R. Gillian & C.G. Mascie-Taylor (Eds.), *Infertility in the modern world. Present and future prospects* (pp. 238-260).Cambridge: Cambridge University Press.

Patterson, C.J. (2001). Families of the lesbian baby boom: Maternal mental health and child adjustment. In D. F. Glazer & J. Drescher (Eds.), *Gay and lesbian parenting* (pp. 91-108). New York: The Haworth Press, Inc.

Patterson, C.J. (2002). Children of lesbian and gay parents: research, law, and policy. In B.L. Bottoms, M. Bull Kovera & B.D. McAuliff (Eds.), *Children, social science, and the law* (pp. 176-199). Cambridge: Cambridge University Press.

Picavet, H. S. J. (2001). National health surveys by mail or home interview: effects on response. *Journal of Epidemiology and Community Health, 55*, 408-413.

Rand, C., Graham, D. & Rawlings, E. (1982). Psychological health and factors the court seeks to control in lesbian mother custody trails. *Journal of Homosexuality, 8*, 27-39.

Robbroeckx, L. M. H., & Wels, P. M. A. (1989). *Nijmeegse vragenlijst voor de opvoedingssituatie (NVOS) [Nijmegen questionnaire regarding child rearing circumstances]*. Nijmegen: Instituut voor orthopedagogiek, katholieke Universiteit Nijmegen.

Roberts, W. L. (1986). Nonlinear models of development: An example from the socialization of competence. *Child Development, 57*, 1166-1178.

Roberts, W. L. & Strayer, J. (1987). Parents' responses to the emotional distress of their children: Relations with children's competence. *Developmental Psychology, 23*, 415-422.

Ross, M.W. & Rosser, B. R. (1996). Measurement and correlates of internalized homophobia: A factor analytic study. *Journal of Clinical Psychology, 52*, 15-21.

Rothuizen, J. (2001). Lesbisch ouderschap. In K. A. P. de Bruin & M. Balkema (Eds.), Liever vrouwen. Theorie en praktijk van de lesbisch-specifieke hulpverlening *[Preferably women. Theory and practice of lesbian specific counseling]* (pp.119-136). Amsterdam: Schorer Boeken.

Rowland, R. (1984). Reproductive technologies: the final solution to the woman question. In R. Arditti, R. Duelli Klein & S. Minden (Eds.), *Test-tube women: What future for Motherhood?* (pp. 356-369). London: Pandora Press.

Sandfort, Th. G. M. (1997). *Samen of Apart. Wat homoseksuele mannen en lesbische vrouwen beweegt [Together or separate. Aspects that affect gay men and lesbian women].* Utrecht: Utrecht University, Department of Gay and Lesbian Studies

Sandfort, Th. G. M. (1998). Homosexual and bisexual behavior in European countries. In M. Hubert, N. Bajos & Th. G. M. Sandfort (Eds.), *Sexual behavior and HIV/AIDS in Europe* (pp. 68-106). London: UCL Press.

Sandfort, Th. G. M, & Bos, H. (1998). Homoseksualiteit in gezondheidsperspectief In A. K. Slob, C. W. Vink, J. P. C. Moors & W. Everaerd. *Leerboek seksuologie [Manual of sexology]* (pp. 325-342). Houten: Bohn Staflue Van Loghumn.

Sandfort, Th. G. M. (2000). Homosexuality, psychology, and gay and lesbian studies. In Th. G. M. Sandfort, J. Schuyf, J. W. Duyvendak & J. Weeks (Eds.), *Lesbian and gay studies. An introductory, interdisciplinary approach* (pp. 14-45). London: Sage Publications.

Sandfort. Th. G. M. & Bos, H. (2000). *Being open at work.* Paper presentatie APA congres 2000

Sandfort, Th. G. M., Bos, H. & Vet, R. (in press). Lesbians and gay men at work: Consequences of being out. In A. M. Omoto & H. S. Kurtzman (Eds.), *Sexual orientation, mental health, and substance use: Contemporary scientific perspectives.* London: Sage Publications.

Seccombe, K. (1991). Assessing the costs and benefits of children: gender comparisons among childfree husbands and wives. *Journal of Marriage and the Family, 53,* 191-202.

Seyda, B. & Herrrera, D. (1998). *Women in love. Portraits of lesbian mothers and their families.* Boston: Bulfinch Press Book.

Shidlo, A. (1994). Internalized homophobia: Conceptual and empirical issues in measurement. In R. Greene & G. Herek (Eds.), *Psychological perspectives on lesbian and gay issues: Vol 1. Lesbian and gay psychology: theory, research, and clinical applications* (pp. 176- 205). Thousand Oaks, CA: Sage.

Siemiatycki, J. A. (1979). A comparison of mail, telephone, and home interview strategies for household health surveys. *American Journal of Public Health, 69,* 238- 245.

Simons, R.L. & Associates (1996). Understanding differences between divorced and intact families: stress, interactions, and child outcome. Thousand Oaks, CA: Sage.

Schuijf, J. (1994). *Een stilzwijgende samenzwering. Lesbische vrouwen in Nederland 1920-1970 [ A conspiracy of silence. Lesbian women in the Netherlands 1920-1970].* Leiden: Universiteit Leiden.

Slater, M.A. & Power, T.G. (1987). Multidimensional assessment of parenting in single-Parent families. In J.P. Vincent (Ed.), *Advances in family intervention, assessment and theory. Vol.4* (pp. 197–228). New York: JAI Press.

Slater, S. (1999). *The lesbian family life cycle.* Chicago: University of Illinois Press.

Sociaal cultureel planbureau (2000). *Sociaal en Cultureel Rapport 2000: Nederland en Europa.* Rijswijk: SCP.

Stacey, J., & Biblarz, T. (2001). (How) does the sexual orientation of parents matter?. *American Sociological Review, 66,* 159-183.

Steckel, A. (1987). Psychosocial development of children of lesbian mothers. Gay and lesbian parents. In F. Bozett (Ed.), *Homosexuality and family relations* (pp. 23-36). New York: Harrington Park.

Steenhof, L. & Harmsen. C. (2002). Samenwoners van gelijk geslacht. *Maandstatistiek van de Bevolking [Monthly population statistics], 50,* 4-6.

Steenhof, L. & Harmsen, C. (2003). *Same-sex couples in the Netherlands.* Paper for workshop on comparative research, Rome, Italy, 30 June-2 July 2003.

Stevens, M., Perry, B., Burston, A., Golombok, S. & Golding, J. (2003). Openness in lesbian-mother families regarding mother's sexual orientation and child's conception by donor insemination. *Journal of Reproductive and Infant Psychology, 21,* 347-362.

Stryker, S. & Statham, A. (1985). Symbolic interaction and role theory. In G. Lindzey & E. Aronson (Eds.), *Handbook of social psychology* (pp. 311-378). New York: Random House.

Sullivan, M. (1996). Rozzie and Hariet? Gender and family patters of lesbian coparents. *Gender and Society,10,* 747-767.

Szymanski, D.M., Chung, B. & Balsam, K. F. (2001). Psychosocial correlates of internalized homophobia in lesbians. *Measurement and evaluation in counseling and development, 34,* 27-38.

Tasker, F. L. & Golombok, S. (1995). Adults raised as children in lesbian families. *American Journal of Orthopsychiatry, 65,* 203-215.

Tasker, F. L. & Golombok, S. (1997). *Growing up in a lesbian family*. London, Guilford Press.

Ten Haaf, P.G.J., Janssen, J.M.A.M. & Gerris, J.R.M. (1994). Child rearing meausures: Convergent and scriminant validity. *European Journal of Psychological Assessment, 10*, 111-128.

Thompson, C. M. (2002) Fertile ground: Feminists theorize infertility. In M.C. Inhorn & F. Van Balen (Eds.), *Infertility around the globe. New thinking on childlessness, gender, and reproductive technologies* (pp. 52-78).Berkeley: University of California Press.

Thompson, J. M. (2002). *Mommy queerest*. Massachusetts, University of Massachusetts Press.

Touroni, E. & Coyle, A. (2002). Decision-making in planned lesbian parenting: An interpretative phenomenological analysis. *Journal of Community and Applied Social Psychology, 12*, 194-209.

Trickett, P. K. & Susman, E. J. (1988). Parental perception of child rearing practices in physically abusive and nonabusive families. *Developental Psychology, 24*, 270-276.

Ulrich, M. & Weatherall, A. (2000). Motherhood and infertility. Viewing motherhood through the lens of infertility. *Feminism and Psychology, 10*, 323-336.

Van Balen, F. & Trimbos-Kemper, T. C. M. J. (1995). Involuntarily childless couples. Their desire to have children and their motives. *Journal of Psychosomatic Obstetrics and Gynaecology, 16*, 137-144.

Van Balen, F. (1996). Child rearing following In Vitro Fertilization. *Journal of Child Psychology and Psychiatry, 37*, 687-693.

Van Balen, F. (1998). Development of IVF Children. *Developmental Review, 18*, 30-46.

Van Balen, F. & Inhorn, M. (2002) Introduction. Interpreting infertility: A view from the social sciences. In M.C. Inhorn & F. Van Balen (Eds.), *Infertility around the globe. New thinking on childlessness, gender, and reproductive technologies* (pp. 3-32). Berkeley: University of California Press.

Van de Meerendonk, B. & Scheepers, P. (in press). Denial of equal rights for lesbians and gay men.

Van der Avort, A., Cuyvers P. & De Hoog, K. (1996). *Het Nederlandse gezinsleven aan het eind van de twintigste eeuw [Dutch family live at the end of the 20th century]*. Den Haag: Nederlandse Gezinsraad.

Vanfraussen K., Ponjaert-Kristoffersen I. & Brewaeys, A. (2001). An attempt to reconstruct children's donor concept: A comparison between children's and lesbian parent's attitudes towards donor anonymity. *Human Reproduction, 16*, 2019-2025.

Vanfraussen, K., Ponjaert- Kristoffersen, I. & Brewaeys, A. (2002). What does it mean for youngster to grow up in a lesbian family created by means of donor insemination? *Journal of Reproductive and Infant Psychology, 20*, 237-252.

Vanfraussen, K., Pontjaert-Kristoffersen, I. & Brewaeys, A. (2003). Family functioning in lesbian families created by donor insemination. *American Journal of Orthopsychiatry, 73*, 78-90.

Verhulst, F., Van Den Ende, J. & Koot, H. (1996). *Manual for the Dutch version of the child behavior checklist/ 4-18*. Rotterdam: University of Rotterdam, Department of Child Psychiatry.

Vermulst, A. A., Gerris, J. R. M. & Siebenheller, F. A. (1987). *Opvoedingsdoelen. Bepaling van de onderliggende betekenisdimensies in het meetinstrument opvoedingsdoelen m.b.v. een drietal multivariate analysestechnieken [Child rearing goals. Measurement of Significant dimensions in the Child rearing Goals List by means of three multivariate techniques]*. Amsterdam: Vakgroep Algemene Pedagogiek.

Waaldijk, K. (1993). The legal situation in the member states. In K. Waalwijk & A. Clapham (Eds.), *Homosexuality: A European community Issue* (pp. 130-138). Dordrecht: Martinus Nijhoff.

Waldo, C.R. (1999). Working in a majority context: A structural model of heterosexism as minority stress in the workplace. *Journal of Counseling Psychology, 46*, 218-232.

Wardle, L. D. (1997). The potential impact of homosexual parenting on children. *University of Illinois Law Review*, 833-919.

Warmerdam, H. & Gort, A. (1998). *Meer dan gewenst. Handboek voor lesbische en homoseksuele ouders [More than wished for. Handbook for lesbian and gay parents]*. Amsterdam: Schorer Boeken.

Weeda, I. (1989) Enquête moederschap, hoe denken Nederlandse en Opzij- vrouwen over kinderen. *Opzij, 8*, 24-31.

Weeks, J., Heaphy, B. & Donovan, C. (2001). *Same- sex intimacies. Families of choice and other life experiments*. London: Routledge.

Weinraub, M. & Wolf, B. (1983). Effects of stress and social supports and two- parent families. *Child Development, 54*, 1297-1311.

Wels, P. M. A., & Robbroeckx, L. M. H. (1991). Gezinsbelasting en hulpverlening aan gezinnen II, de constructie van de Nijmeegse vragenlijst voor opvoedingssituatie. *Tijdschrift voor Orthopedagogiek, 30*, 63-79.

Wendland, C. L., Byrn, F., & Hill, C. (1996). Donor insemination: A comparison of lesbian couples, heterosexual couples and single women. *Fertility and Sterility, 65*, 764-770.

Werner, E.E. & Smith, R.S. (1982). *Vulnerable but invincible: A longitudinal study of reslient children and youth.* New York: McGraw Hill.

Weston, K. (1991). *Families we choose: Lesbians, gays, and kinships.* New York: Columbia University Press.

Widmer, E. D., Treas, J, & Newcomb, R. (1998). Attitudes toward non- marital sex in 24 countries. *Journal of Sex Research, 35*, 349-358.

Youniss, J. & Smollar, S (1985). *Adolescent relationships with mothers, fathers and friends.* Chicago: Chicago University Press.Widmer, E. D., Treas, J. & Newcomb, R. (1998). Attitudes toward non- marital sex in 24 countries. Journal of Sex Research, 35, 349-358.

# Summary

This thesis reports on a study on lesbian families in which the children were born to the lesbian relationship. In the literature, such families are called 'planned lesbian families,' because they consist of two lesbian women who decided to have their children together, in contrast to lesbian families in which the children were born in previous heterosexual relationship. The focus is on what it means to be a lesbian mother, and what it means for children to grow up in a planned lesbian family. For example, how strong is the desire of lesbian mothers to have a child, and what are their motivations? How do lesbian mothers experience parenthood? What do they strive for in child rearing? How do they experience the relationship with their partner, and do they feel supported by others? What is the quality of the parent-child relationship in lesbian families? Do lesbian mothers feel rejected, and if so, does this have a negative impact on their role as a parent, and does it negatively influence child adjustment? Scientific inquiries into most of these issues are lacking. The study reported on here compared 100 two-mother families with 100 heterosexual families, and is the largest study on planned lesbian families to date.

Chapter I describes the background and aim of the investigations, and stresses the importance of research on a relatively new phenomenon that planned lesbian families are. Chapter II provides an overview of previous studies on lesbian parenthood. Based on this, research questions on lesbian families are formulated. Inquiries on lesbian families can be broken down into two phases. In the first phase, systematic studies of lesbian families focused on lesbian families having children born in a previous heterosexual relationship. In the second phase, the studies included lesbian families whose children were born to the lesbian couple. Studies in both phases emphasized that lesbian parents and their children are very similar to heterosexual parents raising children. By emphasizing this similarity, research failed to elucidate family processes in which lesbian and heterosexual families differ, such as the desire and motivation to have children, the pressure to be a 'good mom,' and the division of family tasks. Lesbian as well as heterosexual families could differ on these aspects, due to their special circumstances. Another issue pointed out in Chapter II is that although family functioning in lesbian families might be just as varied, challenging, comforting, amusing, and frustrating as it is in heterosexual families, it is the stigma of lesbianism and the lack of acknowledgement of lesbian families that make their family life different.

Chapter III presents the results of a study on the motivation to have a child among lesbian mothers compared to heterosexual parents. It was found that happiness is more important for lesbian mothers than it is for heterosexual parents, and that identity development is less important for lesbian mothers than it is for heterosexual parents. On the other hand, the hierarchy of motivations for lesbian as well as heterosexual parents is quite similar. The desire to have children appears to be stronger in lesbian parents than in heterosexual parents, and the former tend to spend more time thinking about their motives for having children.

Chapter IV presents the findings of an investigation on experiences of parenthood, child rearing goals, couple relationship, and social support in lesbian parents compared to heterosexual parents. Only a few differences were established. Conformity as a child rearing goal is less important to biological and social mothers than it is to heterosexual parents. Lesbian social mothers more often feel the need to justify the quality of their parenthood, compared to fathers in heterosexual families. Finally, lesbian parents are neither less competent, nor more burdened than heterosexual parents are.

Chapter V focuses on the differences between lesbian and heterosexual families with regard to family characteristics, parental behavior, and child adjustment. Lesbian social mothers report differences in family characteristics and in parental behavior other than those reported by heterosexual fathers. Compared to heterosexual fathers, lesbian social mothers feel more often that they have to justify the quality of parenthood, found traditional child rearing goals less important, and spend more time on family tasks. Lesbian social mothers were found to report more parental concern and emotional involvement than heterosexual fathers. Lesbian mothers used, compared to heterosexual fathers, more induction, showed more respect for the child's autonomy. However, they less often used power assertion and showed less often structure and limit-setting, than heterosexual fathers. Further analyses, however, showed that characteristics that are more or less related to their position as a social mother (for example: parental justification) mediate most of the observed differences between lesbian social mothers and heterosexual fathers in parental behavior. No differences between the psychological adjustment of children in lesbian and those in heterosexual families were established.

In Chapter VI, the focus is on heterogeneity within planned lesbian families with regard to minority stress, and the relation with experiences of parenthood and child adjustment. Minority stress is defined as experiences with negative attitudes regarding the non-traditional family situation of lesbian mothers, and their own attitude toward being a lesbian. It was found that minority stress leads to more parental stress in general and more parental justification. Lesbian mothers with more experiences of rejection reported more behavior problems in their children.

In sum, the findings show that lesbian families differ from heterosexual families in several respects. Lesbian social mothers and heterosexual fathers differ in the

strength of the desire to have a child, in child rearing goals, and in the valuation of the relationship with their child. Lesbian social mothers and heterosexual fathers also differ in parental behavior. The observed differences do not originate solely from gender, the position of lesbian social mothers in society, and/or the absence or presence of a biological link. It revealed that these variables create a different kind of family structure that has consequences for the quality of the parent-child relationship.

The findings emphasize the importance of the effect of minority stress on the lives of lesbian mothers and their children. A task for future research is to examine how children in planned lesbian families cope with being a member of a minority group once they reach puberty. This is an important issue, because the families involved in this thesis will go through other developmental stages in the future, which might lead to changes in family functioning. Coping strategies of lesbian mothers and their children with their minority status is also an important issue for future research because recent publications indicate that the relative acceptance of a lesbian or gay lifestyle in the Netherlands is not a stable situation (NVIH/COC, 2003; Dutch Ministry of Health, Welfare and Sport, 2001).

# Curriculum Vitae

Henny Bos was born in 1963, in Valkenswaard, the Netherlands. After graduating in Educational Sciences from Utrecht University, she worked under the supervision of Theo Sandfort as a research assistant and junior researcher at the Department of Gay and Lesbian Studies at Utrecht University and the Rutger NISSO Group. The focus of research was on gay and lesbian health issues, and on homosexuality in the workplace.

The past four years, Henny Bos was employed at the Department of Education of the Faculty of Social and Behavioural Science of the University of Amsterdam, where she carried out her PhD research on parenting in lesbian families, under the supervision of Frank van Balen and Dymph van den Boom. The research was funded by the Netherlands Organization for Scientific Research.

While working on her PhD, Henny Bos published on homosexuality in the workplace and co-edited the book *Van Adoptie tot Eiceldonatie. Op zoek naar oplossingen voor onvruchtbaarheid* ('From Adoption to Oocyte Donation: Solutions for Infertility'). She is a member of various scientific organizations, including the Nederlandse Vereniging van Seksuologie (Dutch Association of Sexologists) and the Studiegroep Onderzoek Reproduktieve Technieken (Reproductive Techniques Research Study Group), for which she organized several conferences. She guest editor of a special issue of *Patient, Education, and Counseling* ('Infertility, and treatment: The contrast between developing countries and Western welfare states'), and the *Journal of Reproduction and Infant Psychology* ('Infertility, culture, and psychology in worldwide perspective').

In July 2004, she was appointed as a postdoctoral fellow at the University of Amsterdam, where she is now working on a project called 'Child Development in Planned Lesbian Families,'a longitudinal follow-up of the study reported on in this thesis.

# List of publications

## Publications based on the studies described in thesis

Bos, H. M. W., Van Balen, F. & Van Den Boom, D. C. (2004). Experience of parenthood, couple relationship, social support, and child rearing goals in planned lesbian families. *Journal of Child Psychology and Psychiatry, 45*, 755-764.

Bos, H. M. W., Van Balen, F. & Van Den Boom, D.C. (2003). Planned lesbian families: their desire and motivation to have children. *Human Reproduction, 18*, 2216-2224.

Bos, H. M. W., Van Balen, F., Sandfort, Th. G. M. & Van Den Boom, D. C. (in press). Minority stress, experience of parenthood, and child adjustment in lesbian families. *Journal of Reproductive and Infant Psychology.*

Bos, H. M. W., Van Balen, F. & Van Den Boom, D. C. Lesbian Families and Family Functioning: An overview. (In press). *Patiënt Education and Counselling.*

Bos, H. M. W., Van Balen, F. & Van Den Boom, D. C. Family characteristics, child rearing and child adjustment in planned lesbian families. Submitted.

Bos, H. M. W., Van Balen, F. & Van Den Boom, D. C. The distribution of family tasks in planned lesbian families. A comparison with heterosexual families. Submitted.

Bos, H. M. W & Van Balen, F. (2002). Kinderwens en gezinsleven in lesbische gezinnen. In F. van Balen, D. van Berkel, H. M. W,. Bos, Y. De Roode & J. Verdurmen (Eds.), *Van adoptie tot eiceldonatie, op zoek naar oplossingen voor onvruchtbaarheid* (pp. 105-132). Nijkerk: Van Brug.

## Other publications

Sandfort, Th. G. M., Bos, H. & Vet, R. (in press). Lesbians and gay men at work: Consequences of being out. In A. M. Omoto & H. S. Kurtzman (Eds.), *Sexual orientation, mental health, and substance use: Contemporary scientific perspectives.* London: Sage Publications.

Van Balen, F., Van Berkel, D., Bos, H. M.W., De Roode, Y. & Verdurmen, J. (2002). *Van adoptie tot eiceldonatie, op zoek naar oplossingen voor onvruchtbaarheid.* Nijkerk: Van Brug.

Bos, H. & Sandfort, Th. G. M. (1999). *Homoseksuele mannen en vrouwen over hun werksituatie. 'De prijs die ik betaal'* Zoetermeer: ABVAKABO FNV.

Bos, H., Dietz, I., Oudheusden, M. & Sandfort. Th. (1999). Psychosociale problemen bij homoseksuele mannen en lesbische vrouwen: Een vergelijking met heteroseksuelen. *Tijdschrift voor de Seksuologie, 23*, 84-90.

Sandfort, Th. G. M., & Bos, H. (1998). *Sexual preference and work. This is what makes the difference.* Zoetermeer: ABVAKABO FNV.

Bos, H. & Sandfort. Th. (1998). Seksualiteit in Nederland vanuit Europees perspectief. *Tijdschrift voor de Seksuologie, 22*, 11-21

Sandfort, Th. & Bos, H. (1998). Homoseksualiteit in gezondheidsperspectief. In K. Slob, C.W. Vink, J.P. Moors & W. Everaerd (red.), *Leerboek seksuologie.* Houten: Bohn Stafleu Van Loghum.

Sandfort, Th, Bos, H., Haavia-Mannila, E. & Sundet, J.M. (1998). Sexual Practices and their social profiles. In M. Hubert, N. Bajos & Th. Sandfort (Eds.), *Sexual behavior and HIV/AIDS in Europe* (pp. 106-164). Londen: UCL Press.

Sandfort, Th., Hubert, M., Bajos, N. & Bos, H. (1998). Sexual Behavior and HIV Risk: Common Patterns and Differences between European Countries. In M. Hubert, N. Bajos & Th. Sandfort (Eds.), *Sexual behavior and HIV/AIDS in Europe* (pp.403-426). Londen: UCL Press.

Bos, H., Sandfort, Th., Hubert, M. & Bajos, N. (1998). Seksueel gedrag in Nederland en diverse Europese landen. *Tijdschrift voor Seksuologie, 1*,11-21.

Sandfort, Th. & Bos, H. (1997). Waar komen we vandaan, waar gaan we naar toe? Over de oorzaak van homoseksualiteit en waarom we dat willen weten. *Antenne, 16*,4-12.

Warszawski, J. & Bos, H. (1997). Self-reported STD's in various European countries. In: J. van Bergen, O.P. Bleker & M.C.A. van der Brugt (red.) *STD-bulletin; special issue*, 18. Utrecht: Stichting soa-bestrijding.

Warszawski, J. & Bos H. (1997). Zelf rapportage van SOA's in Europese landen. In: J. van Bergen, O.P. Bleker & M.C.A. van der Brugt (red.) *STD-bulletin; special issue*, 18. Utrecht: Stichting soa-bestrijding.

Stroes, F , Bos, H. & Sandfort, Th. (1994). *Lesbische vrouwen en AIDS. Van solidariteit naar persoonlijke bezorgdheid*. Utrecht. Homostudies/ Universiteit Utrecht.

# Samenvatting

Dit proefschrift handelt over lesbische gezinnen waarin de kinderen geboren zijn binnen een lesbische relatie. In de Engelstalige literatuur worden deze gezinnen ook wel 'planned lesbian families' genoemd. Hiermee wordt benadrukt dat in deze gezinnen twee lesbische vrouwen samen voor een kind kiezen. Dit in tegenstelling tot lesbische gezinnen waar het kind geboren is binnen een heteroseksuele relatie van één van de moeders voordat deze een lesbische identiteit aannam ('coming out'). In dit proefschrift is onderzocht wat het betekent om een lesbische moeder te zijn en wat het voor kinderen betekent om op te groeien in een gezin met twee moeders. Waarom kiezen lesbische vrouwen voor kinderen? Ervaren lesbische vrouwen het ouderschap anders dan heteroseksuele ouders en gaan ze op een andere manier met hun kinderen om? Hoe reageert de omgeving (positief, negatief) en wat voor consequenties heeft dit voor ouders en kinderen? Deze vragen komen in 'Parenting in Lesbian Families' aan de orde. In dit proefschrift worden ouderschap, opvoeden en de ontwikkeling van het kind in 100 lesbische gezinnen onderzocht en vergeleken met 100 heteroseksuele gezinnen.

In hoofdstuk I worden de achtergronden en doelen van dit proefschrift besproken en is het belang van studies naar lesbisch ouderschap – hetgeen een relatief nieuw fenomeen is - uiteengezet.

Hoofdstuk II geeft een overzicht van reeds uitgevoerde empirische onderzoeken naar lesbisch ouderschap. Op basis van dit overzicht zijn nieuwe onderzoeksvragen voor dit proefschrift geformuleerd.

In dit hoofdstuk worden in de onderzoeken die tot nu toe verricht zijn naar lesbisch ouderschap twee fases onderscheiden. De eerste fase betreft gezinnen waar de kinderen geboren zijn binnen een heteroseksuele relatie van één van de moeders. De tweede fase betreft gezinnen waar de kinderen geboren zijn binnen de lesbische relatie. In beide fases benadrukken onderzoekers dat lesbische ouders en hun kinderen niet verschillen van heteroseksuele ouders en hun kinderen. Door de overeenkomst tussen lesbische gezinnen en heteroseksuele gezinnen te benadrukken, is er tot nu toe niet onderzocht op welke aspecten beide typen gezinnen van elkaar verschillen. Bijvoorbeeld: de sterkte van de kinderwens, het nadenken over de kinderwens en de motivatie om een kind te wensen, de druk om een 'goede moeder te zijn' en de verdeling tussen zorg en arbeid tussen beide ouders. Lesbische gezinnen verschillen mogelijkerwijs van heteroseksuele gezinnen op deze aspecten met name vanwege hun uitzonderingspositie als minderheid.

Lesbisch ouderschap mag dan wel even gevarieerd, uitdagend en belastend zijn als in heteroseksuele gezinnen maar in tegenstelling tot heteroseksuele gezinnen krijgen lesbische ouders vooral te maken met stigmatisering. Dit maakt dat hun gezinsleven anders wordt dan dat van heteroseksuelen.

In hoofdstuk III worden de resultaten beschreven van de studie waarin ouderschaps-motieven en sterkte van de kinderwens van lesbische ouders vergeleken worden met die van heteroseksuele ouders. In vergelijking met heteroseksuele vaders en moeders, zijn motieven op het gebied van geluk voor lesbische moeders belangrijker. Daarentegen zijn voor lesbische moeders motieven op het terrein van identiteit minder belangrijk. De rangorde van de motieven is voor lesbische en heteroseksuele ouders identiek. Lesbische ouders hebben echter een sterkere kinderwens en besteden meer tijd aan het nadenken over de kinderwens in vergelijking met heteroseksuele ouders.

In hoofdstuk IV zijn de resultaten gepresenteerd van de studie waarin lesbische ouders vergeleken worden met heteroseksuele ouders ten aanzien van de ervaring met ouderschap, de opvoedingsdoelen die zij hebben, hun relatiesatisfactie en de sociale steun die zij ontvangen. Het blijkt dat lesbische en heteroseksuele ouders slechts op een aantal van deze aspecten van elkaar verschillen. Biologische moeders en sociale moeders (de moeder die het kind niet gebaard heeft) hechten minder belang aan traditionele opvoedingsdoelen dan heteroseksuele ouders. Lesbische, sociale moeders hebben vaker het gevoel dat zij de kwaliteit van hun ouderschap moeten verdedigen/ bewijzen in vergelijking met vaders in heteroseksuele gezinnen. Tenslotte vinden lesbische ouders zich even competent in het ouderschap en ondervinden zij ook niet meer stress dan heteroseksuele ouders.

Hoofdstuk V behandelt de verschillen tussen lesbische gezinnen en heteroseksuele gezinnen voor wat betreft gezinskenmerken, ouderlijk gedrag en het welbevinden van de kinderen. Lesbische sociale moeders verschillen van heteroseksuele vaders op verschillende gezinskenmerken en ouderlijk gedrag. In vergelijking met heteroseksuele vaders, vinden lesbische, sociale moeders vaker dat zij de kwaliteit van hun ouderschap moeten verdedigen/bewijzen. Zij hanteren minder traditionele opvoedingsdoelen en besteden meer tijd aan taken in het gezin. Lesbische sociale moeders rapporteren ook meer bezorgdheid over en emotionele betrokkenheid bij de opvoeding dan heteroseksuele vaders. Lesbische ouders geven, in vergelijking met heteroseksuele vaders, vaker aan gebruik te maken van inductie tijdens de opvoeding (het kind wijzen op gevolgen van gedrag, praten met het kind en het kind wijzen op eerder gemaakte afspraken) en respecteren de autonomie van het kind meer. Daarentegen geven zij, in vergelijking met heteroseksuele vaders, minder vaak aan in de opvoeding gebruik te maken van straf en bieden minder structuur aan in de ouder-kind interactie. Aanvullende analyses laten zien dat de verschillen in ouderschapsgedragingen tussen de lesbische, sociale moeder en heteroseksuele vader met name gemedieerd worden door kenmerken die min of meer verbonden zijn met de positie van de sociale moeder (bijvoorbeeld: bewijzen/ verdedigen van haar kwaliteiten als ouder). Er zijn geen verschillen gevonden tussen kinderen in lesbische gezinnen en heteroseksuele gezinnen ten aanzien van welbevinden.

Hoofdstuk VI gaat over (a) negatieve ervaringen als gevolg van de niet-traditionele levensstijl van de lesbische moeders en (b) (negatieve) attitudes die de vrouwen hebben ten aanzien van hun eigen seksuele oriëntatie. In de Engelstalige literatuur worden deze negatieve ervaringen en attitudes samengevat met de term 'minority stress'. Resultaten wijzen erop dat lesbische moeders die minority stress ervaren, het ouderschap meer als stressvol ervaren en ook vaker het idee hebben zich als ouder te moeten bewijzen. Lesbische vrouwen die vaker geconfronteerd werden met (negatieve) uitlatingen rondom hun (niet-traditionele) leefsituatie rapporten meer gedragsproblemen bij hun kinderen.

Samenvattend blijkt het dat lesbische gezinnen op een aantal aspecten van heteroseksuele gezinnen verschillen. Lesbische, sociale moeders en heteroseksuele vaders verschillen, van elkaar in de sterkte van de kinderwens, de opvoedingsdoelen en de wijze waarop zij de ouder-kind relatie ervaren. Zij verschillen ook van elkaar in ouderschapsgedragingen. De gevonden verschillen tussen lesbische, sociale moeders en heteroseksuele vaders zijn niet alleen toe te schrijven aan het sekseverschil. De positie van de lesbische, sociale moeder in onze samenleving, maar ook de afwezigheid van een biologische band van deze moeder met het kind kunnen hierbij een rol spelen. Het is aannemelijk dat door deze aspecten een gezinsstructuur ontstaat die anders is dan in heteroseksuele gezinnen en die van invloed is op de kwaliteit van de ouder-kind relatie.

De resultaten tonen tevens aan dat 'minority stress' van invloed kan zijn op het leven van lesbische moeders en hun kinderen. Toekomstig onderzoek zou zich moeten richten op de vraag hoe de kinderen in lesbische gezinnen - met name tijdens de adolescentie - omgaan met de niet-traditionele gezinssituatie en het feit dat ze behoren tot een minderheidsgroep. Dit is van belang, omdat met het ouder worden van deze kinderen de gezinnen ook in een andere ontwikkelingsfase komen, hetgeen gepaard kan gaan met veranderingen in het functioneren van het gezin. Een andere reden waarom dit onderwerp van belang is, volgt uit recente publicaties die aangeven dat de acceptatie van lesbische vrouwen en homoseksuele mannen in Nederland instabiel is (NVIH/COC, 2003; Dutch Ministry of Health, Welfare and Sport, 2001).

# Dankwoord

Diverse instanties en mensen hebben op verschillende manieren en tijdstippen een bijdrage geleverd bij het tot stand komen van dit proefschrift. Een opsomming hiervan is bijna onmogelijk. Ik ga toch een poging wagen, want aan al die instanties en mensen ben ik dank verschuldigd.

Zo zijn daar instellingen die mij geholpen hebben bij het werven van lesbische gezinnen, zoals Stichting Medisch Centrum voor Geboorteregeling en de landelijke homo ouder groep 'Meer dan gewenst' van N.V.I.H./C.O.C. Ambtenaren van de afdeling Bevolking van verschillende gemeenten en de leiding van diverse scholen, hebben hulp geboden bij het benaderen van heteroseksuele gezinnen. En dan zijn daar natuurlijk de (ex-) studenten (Sandra Rison, Floor van Rooij, Wendy Tieman, Irmi Mauer, Caroline van der Haven, Astrid Bollebakker en Meintje Schrauwers) die reddende engelen waren in de fases van dataverzameling en scoring van het observatie materiaal. Bij de mensen van het secretariaat kon ik altijd even mijn ei kwijt als ik toe was aan een 'loopje'. In dit rijtje horen ook mijn collega aio's en dan met name zij die in dezelfde periode zijn begonnen, zoals Mirjam Gevers Deynoot-Schaub, Ellen Reitz (inmiddels postdoc), Miriam Fossen, Marjolijn Blom en mijn Utrecht-Amsterdam (visa versa) reismaatje Jochem Thijs. Dank ook aan al die mensen die tegen mij zijn blijven zeggen dat ik ook aan mijn sociale leven moest denken, zoals Anja van Belkum en mijn paranimfen Eus Davies en Liesbeth van Doorn. Maar ook dank aan de verschillende eetclubjes waarmee ik regelmatig rond te tafel zit (Gio en Saskia, Rudolf, de 'Mollergirls' en de Utrechtse meidenclub) en de spelletjesclub bij Joep en Frieda. Bij mijn buren Jo ter Beeke en Ronald de Klein en hun kinderen Anne en Dana kon ik dikwijls zo maar aanschuiven om mee te eten (of bioscoopje pikken, voetbal kijken, enz.) Inhoudelijke uitwisselingen heb ik de afgelopen 4 jaren met name gehad met mijn collega's van de leerstoel Opvoeding en Opvoedingsondersteuning. De OOS mensen waren met name van belang voor de wetenschappelijke dialoog als het over kinderen en opvoeding ging. Mensen van de Schorerstichting (onder andere Josee Rothuizen) en oud collega's/vrienden van de Rutger Nisso Groep (met name Charles Picavet) waren vooral van belang als het ging om mijn gedachtes aan te scherpen als het ging om homoseksualiteit, lesbische vrouwen en lesbische moeders.

Er zijn een aantal personen die bij het werken aan dit onderzoek, maar ook in de aanloop hiertoe, van grote betekenis voor mij zijn geweest. Deze mensen wil ik hier persoonlijk 'toespreken' en bedanken. Om te beginnen wil ik noemen mijn promotor Dymph van den Boom en copromotor Frank van Balen. Dymph, je was altijd kritisch op de stukken die ik bij je afleverde (met echte rode strepen door de teksten), maar ik denk dat ik een enorme goede leerschool bij je heb gehad. Ik ben dan ook erg blij dat je bij het vervolg project betrokken wilt blijven. Frank van Balen was degene met wijze raad en heeft mij ontzettend veel kansen gegeven. Frank, ik waardeer het zeer dat je ook tijdens de misschien wel moeilijkste periode in je leven mij bent blijven begeleiden. En zoals je het kort geleden tijdens het congres in Sheffield nog zo mooi formuleerde: ja, wij zijn een goed team. Ik heb jarenlang nog met iemand anders een goed team gevormd (en naar ik hoop nog steeds) en dat is Theo Sandfort. Theo, ik heb je het al meerdere malen gezegd: de kansen die jij mij hebt gegeven en de tijd die jij in mij geïnvesteerd hebt zijn van groot belang geweest. Pap ('mijn persoonlijke adviseur') en mam ('casa mama' als ik me vrijwillig wil opsluiten om een deadline te halen) in dit rijtje horen jullie ook thuis. Mijn keuzes zijn misschien niet altijd de meest logische geweest, maar jullie hebben er altijd weer energie in gestopt om ze te begrijpen. Tot op de dag van vandaag blijven jullie belangstelling hebben in mijn leven en werk.

Naast deze personen dank ik ook NWO die door het verstrekken van subsidie de uitvoering van dit onderzoek mogelijk heeft gemaakt. En tot slot natuurlijk dank aan al de 100 lesbische en 100 heteroseksuele gezinnen. De bezoekjes aan jullie waren onvergetelijk! En zonder de tijd en energie die jullie in het onderzoek hebben gestoken was dit proefschrift nooit mogelijk geweest. Dank hiervoor!

Henny Bos
Amsterdam, 14 september 2004